How You

Can Help Change

the World

Spiritualizing the World, vol 1

How You

Can Help Change

the World

KIM MICHAELS

Copyright © 2015 Kim Michaels. All rights reserved. No part of this book may be used, reproduced, translated, electronically stored or transmitted by any means except by written permission from the publisher. A reviewer may quote brief passages in a review.

MORE TO LIFE PUBLISHING

www.morepublish.com

For foreign and translation rights,

contact info@ morepublish.com

ISBN: 978-87-93297-06-7

The information and insights in this book should not be considered as a form of therapy, advice, direction, diagnosis, and/or treatment of any kind. This information is not a substitute for medical, psychological, or other professional advice, counseling and care. All matters pertaining to your individual health should be supervised by a physician or appropriate health-care practitioner. No guarantee is made by the author or the publisher that the practices described in this book will yield successful results for anyone at any time. They are presented for informational purposes only, as the practice and proof rests with the individual.

For more information: *www.ascendedmasterlight.com and www.transcendencetoolbox.com*

CONTENTS

Introduction 7
1 | The Energetic Cause of World Events 11
2 | How to Transform Fear-Based Energy 31
3 | Your Life's Purpose 47
4 | A Closer Look at Ascended Masters 57
5 | Why Invoking Spiritual Light Works 73
6 | How to Invoke Spiritual Light 85
7 | Understanding the Planetary Dynamic 91
8 | The Effect of Invoking Spiritual Light 103
9 | Why Invoking Spiritual Light Is so Important 113
10 | Taking Responsibility for Your Planet 135
11 | Overcoming the Sense of Being Powerless 145
12 | You Are Consciousness Looking at Itself 157
13 | The Relationship Between People and Planet 171
14 | Using the Invocations 181
15 | Invoking Light Into the Physical Octave 183
16 | Invoking Light Into the Emotional Octave 201
17 | Invoking Light Into the Mental Octave 221
18 | Invoking Light Into the Identity Octave 239

INTRODUCTION

The books in this series are for people who have an inner knowing, an intuitive sense, of the following:

- My life has a specific, personal purpose. I have a mission on this planet.

- I am not here to leave this planet as I found it. I am here to make a difference, to leave the world in a better condition than when I came.

When you look back at your life, you have probably experienced certain situations or witnessed world events and had a strong inner urge to do something about it. You have always known that there are many things that simply are not right, that really should not be happening on this planet. You have probably also felt powerless because what can one person do about world events?

After reading this book, you will no longer feel powerless. On the contrary, you are likely to feel that for the first time in your life you can clearly see how to fulfill your deep inner longing to do something positive for this planet. You may even have a clear vision of why you came to earth in the first place.

The purpose of this book is to help you get a clearer vision of your mission and introduce you to a set of powerful tools whereby you can make a decisive difference. The following books in the series will give you tools for producing change in specific areas of life.

This book will give you a brief explanation of how the world works. Once you know the underlying mechanism (that none of us learned in school or Sunday School), you will see that even though an individual person may seem insignificant in the face of planetary problems, there is always *something* we can do to make a difference. You have the potential to have a significant positive impact on the future of the planet and society. If you make use of that opportunity, you will make a real contribution. If enough people do the same, we will together make a decisive difference.

This is not idealistic thinking or New Age psycho-babble. It is a matter of knowing how the material world works. As you read the book, you will see why we have not been given that knowledge in kindergarten. There are people and forces who aggressively want to prevent us from accepting the potential and the authority we have for bringing about real change on this planet.

You may think that changing the world requires you to go out and perform heroic deeds in some epic battle—or at least do something else physical. This book will in no way discourage you from taking active part in society. It will, however, show you how to have a positive impact on the world without even leaving home.

The tools presented in this book can be applied by virtually anyone. You need no special education, position in society or skills. You need only the willingness to learn something new and apply what you learn. Opening your eyes and your mouth are the most important requirements. If you are willing to do that, you have what it takes to help change the world.

1 | THE ENERGETIC CAUSE OF WORLD EVENTS

Before we can look at the actual tools for changing the world, we need to deal with the blockages most people have towards accepting that such tools exist or that one person can make a difference. I hope you are not one of the people who physically hears voices. When it comes to the topic of changing the world, you might notice some quite persistent "voices" in your head. You may "hear" them in the form of worded thoughts or strong emotions.

The pacifying voices in your head

When I say: "It is possible to change the world," there might be a voice that vehemently denies this and comes up with arguments for why the world is the way it is and why it cannot be changed—at least no by human beings. One may counter this by pointing to the undeniable progress seen in history. Our earliest forefathers lived in caves. When you compare this to modern civilization, it is rather difficult to deny that change has happened. You might argue that change is not the same as progress, but still: Change is possible.

As the next level of argumentation, I can say: "It is possible for a single human being to help change the world." Again, there might be an intense voice that denies this. One can then look at history and see that some individuals have been instrumental in changing the world, perhaps by bringing forth a new idea or invention. One can argue that other individuals have brought forth ideas and organizations that made the world worse, but this still supports the argument that one person can have an impact on the world.

You may now notice another voice arguing that the people who did help change the world were special: "They all had something you don't have. Who are you to think you could do the same? Are you not just a normal human being?" I would then argue that history has many examples of normal human beings making a contribution to changing the world. No dictator could have brought democracy to the world; the people had to take part in it. One of the major causes of progress is a general raising of awareness and knowledge. Any single person who has raised his or her consciousness has made a positive contribution to progress.

I would also raise the question of whether you really are only a "normal" human being or whether you have the potential to be an extra-ordinary human being? I would even pose the question of whether normal human beings are less ordinary than is ordinarily assumed? This book will show you how to become an extra-ordinary human being.

You might notice a voice saying that even if it is possible in principle for you to help change the word, the practical reality is entirely different. The problems of the world are so complex that you would not even be able to understand them. They are

1 | The Energetic Cause of World Events

also so big that nothing you could possibly do would make a difference. "Ha, ha, ha, this is all hopelessly naive; just go back to being ordinary!"

In the rest of this chapter, I will give you an understanding of how the world works that will show you why these voices are wrong. It will also show you why the voices are so desperate to pacify you, even why some forces outside of you are desperate to keep you pacified.

When we begin contemplating the potential for changing the world, the most common initial reaction is that we feel overwhelmed. In order to help you overcome this debilitating feeling, I will give you a simplified explanation of how the world works. When you have the big picture, you can see that it is indeed possible for a single human being to make a real contribution to improving the world.

The wrecking ball room

Let me give you a symbolic illustration of how the world works. Imagine you have to go into a large building in order to get something you need. You walk through a long corridor and come to a set of double doors. As you open one door, you see a large room with a rather chaotic scene. The middle of the room is an area with barriers around it, almost like an ice-hockey rink. On the floor you see a lot of iron balls, about 50 cm in diameter and seemingly quite heavy. They are constantly moving around, bumping into each other and the barriers. At your end of the enclosure is a protected area. A lot of people are standing there, wondering how to get through the wrecking balls in the middle.

As you watch, a person jumps into the fray and tries to run through the balls. He seems to make good progress but is then hit by a ball and knocked out. You then notice some people who have what looks like scientific equipment. As you approach, you realize from their talk that they are studying the balls, seeking to discern patterns for how the balls move. They think that if they can find the underlying pattern, they can either stop the balls, control the balls or help people find a safe passage. They believe that the key to controlling the balls is to study the balls themselves and that there is nothing beneath the floor in the room.

In another corner you see a group of people dressed like priests. As you approach, you realize they claim that the balls behave according to the doctrines of their religion. They claim that if you follow their rules, some day someone will come and take you to the other side. Some of them think they can control the movements of the balls with their prayers.

As you wonder what to do, a thought occurs to you: "What if there is a hidden mechanism that makes the balls move and what if it is below the floor?" You remember that back in the corridor you saw a set of stairs leading down. You decide to go down to see for yourself. As you go down, you come to another large room that is beneath the first one.

In the second room you see a number of electromagnets that are moving around on wheels. Each magnet has a built-in computer that is seemingly programmed to move the magnet in a certain pattern. You realize that each ball on the floor above is being moved around by one electromagnet.

You now see that both the scientists and the religious people cannot ever be successful in their efforts. The key to controlling the balls is not found at the level of the balls. You could run into the arena and try to physically restrict the balls, but one human being is not as strong as an electromagnet. Even collectively, the people would not be able to physically restrict all of the balls.

1 | The Energetic Cause of World Events

It is futile to try to control the balls at the level where you see the balls. The movement of the balls is only an effect of a cause found at the underlying level. You cannot physically overpower the electromagnets, but when you look closer, you see that each magnet has a power supply with an on-off switch. You cannot overpower the magnet, but you can shut off the magnet and thereby take the power away from the ball above it. You realize that there are so many magnets that you cannot turn them all off by yourself. Yet if each person would turn off just one magnet, it would decisively reduce the amount of chaos in the room.

Energy is cause, matter is effect

What does this story tell us about the world and how it works? When we take our inner sense that we are here to improve the world, we tend to think that we have to go out and do something physical in order to change things. We look at some of the physical, material conditions that need to be changed and we think the only way to do so is to change them at the same level where we see them. This is like the people who think they can change the wrecking balls only at the level of the upper floor.

Many spiritually inclined people know war is wrong and many have a sense that we are here to help stop war. When we consider what we might do at the physical level to stop war, the task seems either impossible or overwhelming. What could one human being do physically to stop a problem of the magnitude of war? If we don't stop it physically, what good will it do?

What we can learn from the story is that the level of material conditions and physical actions is not the only level of the world. Even more important, the physical level is not the level of cause. What happens at the physical level is to a large degree the effect of causes that take place at levels that are invisible to our physical senses.

There is a level of the world that is beyond the physical level, and it is what happens here that sets the stage for events at the physical level. We can change what happens at the physical level by changing what happens at the causal level. As we will see, changing what happens at the causal level is far easier than changing things at the physical level.

You might think this sounds too vague and abstract. After all, what proof do I have for this fanciful theory? What I am saying here is not a theory but a simple consequence of what has been proven by science. For more than a century, physicists have had the proof that the physical level is not the level of cause but only the level of effect. Scientists have known that there is a level of cause beyond the material, physical world. I admit that most scientists have not interpreted scientific facts the way I interpret them here, but let us take a closer look at what scientific findings actually mean.

The fact that the physical level is an effect of a deeper cause has been proven by one of the most famous mathematical equations of all time. You have no doubt seen it many times before: $E = mc^2$.

Even mainstream physicists will admit that when you look at the philosophical consequences of this equation, it says that we do not live in the kind of world that our senses and outer minds tell us we live in. What Einstein proved in 1905 is that we do not live in a world that consists of solid matter *and* vibrating energy. Instead, we live in a world that is made entirely of vibrating energy. This conclusion is indisputable and not even the most materialistic scientists can argue against it. What they

1 | The Energetic Cause of World Events

will argue against is when you start making other conclusions based on Einstein's equation, but why should that stop us?

Why does matter appear solid to our physical senses? It is because our senses are calibrated to detect energy vibrations within a certain range or spectrum. We know our ears can hear only certain sounds and that dogs can hear sounds that are inaudible to us. We know our eyes can see only certain types of light and that there are other forms of light that are invisible to us. Matter appears solid to our senses because of the way they are calibrated, but in reality matter is vibrating energy that has been captured (temporarily) into a stationary matrix or field.

When you look at the entire physical planet, all of the matter of which it is made, is vibrating energy. The physical, material world we detect with our senses is only the level of effect. It is made from energy that has been captured in a stationary matrix. The energy was not always trapped in this matrix and it will not remain in that matrix forever. If you could find a way to deal with the energy that makes up matter instead of seeking to change matter through physical means, you could have a far greater impact. Changing the cause is always more powerful than changing the effects.

Which came first: energy or matter?

Before the physical world existed, there was only vibrating energy. This is a consequence of the theory of the Big Bang that is accepted by most scientists. What scientists have not done is to take Einstein's theory further back than the Big Bang. They think it all began with the Big Bang, but this is not what Einstein's equation says. We can show this by playing with the equation as we all learned to do in elementary school.

For example, we can divide with the same factor on both sides of the equal sign. We then get this new version of the equation:

$$\frac{E}{c^2} = \frac{mc^2}{c^2}$$

This is a little messy because c^2 now appears twice on the right side. They eliminate each other and we get a cleaner equation:

$$\frac{E}{c^2} = m$$

This new equation tells us that before the Big Bang (before any mass was created), there was a form of energy. This primordial energy was reduced in vibration by a very large factor and it was this reduction that "created" what we call matter. Matter is a form of energy that is generated by reducing the vibration of a higher form of energy. The primordial energy is cause and what we see as matter is only effect.

Can we prove that this primordial energy exists? That depends on what you mean by proof. Einstein's equation has proven mathematically that there must be a higher form of energy that could be reduced in order to produce the matter we all see. Otherwise matter could not exist. What I have just said above is a logical proof. If you want a physical proof, meaning that scientists create a material instrument that can detect the primordial energy, then you might never get it. How could an instrument created out of the lower vibrations that make up matter ever detect the energies that are far higher than those of matter?

1 | The Energetic Cause of World Events

Einstein chose the value c² because it is a very large number. The primordial energy vibrates at a level that is incredibly high compared to physical matter. Saying we can build an instrument that can detect the energy that existed before the Big Bang is like saying we should be able to build a telescope that can see the farthest regions of the universe—regions from which light has not had time to reach us.

For those who are not lost in wanting a material proof of everything, it is possible to accept the logical conclusion. Cause always comes before effect. There is a level of energy that existed before the physical matter that makes up the world. This level of energy is cause and the level of physical matter is effect. If you really want to change what happens at the physical level, you need to learn how to change what happens at the level of energy. How might we do that?

The real cause of world events

In order to make this less abstract, let us take another look at the problem of war. War is a very physical process. Once physical war has started, it is often very hard to stop. It usually has to run its course until one side accepts defeat or until both sides accept that no one can win and call it a day.

You may have read that World War I was started when a lone gunman assassinated some important person or other. After this "shot heard around the world," physical war broke out and could not be stopped until 17 million deaths and five years later. Some history books admit that this singular assassination was not the cause of the war. They talk about various economic and political factors that had created a situation with "escalating tension" that simply waited for a spark to ignite the explosion. What the history books don't usually do is to consider where this build-up of "escalating tension" might have taken place. With our newfound awareness of energy as cause, we can go beyond the history books.

The escalating tension before the war was created because various groups of people had specific feelings towards each other. These included: fear, anger, mistrust, hatred and blame. According to Einstein, a feeling is a form of energy. This is where we have to confront the prevailing scientific tendency to insist that everything must have a materialistic explanation.

As already mentioned, Einstein proved that there is a form of energy that is far beyond the energy that makes up matter. It is pretty hard to acknowledge this without seeing that the energy that preceded the creation of the matter world is *not* material energy. That which comes first is not created by something that comes later; *cause* is not created by *effect*.

In today's materialistic culture, many scientists insist that matter is cause and mind, including feelings, is effect. They say the gray matter in our brains produces all of our thoughts and feelings. This is neither logical nor is it in line with Einstein's findings. It is not logical to say that the matter in the brain and nervous system can produce all of our thoughts and feelings. Mind is clearly operating with vibrations that are higher than those of physical matter. That which comes before is cause and that which comes after is effect.

When World War I broke out, what came fist? This is not a "chicken-and-egg" type of question. The tension at the emotional level clearly came before any physical actions were taken. Feelings go before actions, and that means physical action is caused by a non-physical feeling. Before we take physical action, there is a build-up of emotional energy. When this energy reaches a certain intensity, it triggers us to take physical action. The build-up of emotional tension in the years before war broke out was the non-physical cause of the physical events of war. Without this build-up of emotional energy, it is possible that physical war would not have been triggered.

After all, war can be life-threatening and people have a survival instinct. Only very powerful emotions can get people to ignore their fear of dying so they are willing to go to war. If you really want to stop war – and numerous other physical events – you need to find out how to deal with energy, meaning mental and emotional energy. If you can stop the build-up of non-physical or psychic energy before it reaches critical mass, you can stop the outbreak of war or other physical events.

The realm of energetic causes

The build-up of emotional tension that sets the stage for physical action must take place in a realm of pure energy, a realm that is beyond what we normally call the material world. Such a realm has been a logical possibility since Einstein. We all learned in school that red light has the lowest vibration of visible light and violet has the highest vibration. We learned that below the vibration of red light is infra-red and above the vibration of violet is ultra-violet.

Is it really such a leap of imagination to accept that there is one, and potentially more than one, "realm" or "octave" beyond the material world? This realm is made up of energy vibrations that are higher (or lower) than those of the physical "octave." This is neither mysticism nor New Age psycho-babble but simply a matter of accepting the logical conclusions of Einstein's discoveries.

When we compare this to what has been discovered by the science of psychology, we can postulate that there is more than one realm beyond the physical. Actions are triggered by strong emotions, but emotions come from thoughts and thoughts come from an even deeper layer of the psyche, namely our sense of identity.

A world event, such as a war, is not caused only by physical conditions (as most historians seem to think). The build-up for war begins in a level of higher energies, namely the level of identity. Before World War I, there was a long-standing conflict between people who identified themselves as Germans, Englishmen, Frenchmen and so on. This sense of identity triggered certain thoughts about why these other nationalities were inferior to your own, how they had wronged you and how they should be forced to change. These thoughts triggered a range of emotions based on fear and anger.

Over many years, this process produced large amounts of psychic energy that gradually accumulated in the emotional, mental and identity realms. When this accumulation of energy passed a critical level, the tension became so overpowering that people's normal drive to avoid war was suspended and nations went to war regardless of their fear of the consequences. The accumulation of energy overpowered people's ability to act rationally.

This raises some questions, such as whether people truly are connected at a level beyond the physical. Again, this will be vehemently denied by materialists, but this denial is no longer sustainable. Einstein's equation says everything is made from energy and energy does not have the same localized properties as what we call matter. The science of quantum physics has conclusively proven that the locality we see at the physical level does not exist at deeper levels. Things only *appear* to be separate but everything is connected at a deeper level. Scientists have also observed numerous examples of a non-physical connection between people or between people and their pets (For more on this, see the book: *The Science Delusion* by Rupert Sheldrake).

We can conclude that all human beings are connected at a higher level of pure energy. We may call it a collective consciousness, perhaps even what Carl Jung called the "collective unconscious." We can now describe this collective consciousness as a realm of emotional energy, a realm of mental energy and a realm of identity energy.

When a world event, such as a war, takes place in the physical realm, it is never just a physical event. It is preceded by a process that takes place in the identity, mental and emotional realms. Physical action is not truly decided at the physical level. It is decided by the process that takes place at the higher levels. When a critical mass of energy has been accumulated, people are often powerless to override the energies. They cannot refuse to act but are pulled into a spiral of violence. We might say that, at the physical level, human beings are merely marionettes. Their strings are pulled by the energies at the three higher levels.

The importance is that if you can stop the build-up of energies before they descend to the physical level, you can stop a certain event. If even a small group of people know how to stop the build-up of fear-based emotional energy, they can prevent certain events from becoming physical. If enough people do this, they can potentially stop all war on this planet. If this seems far-fetched, bear with me until we look at how energy can be changed by anyone willing to apply a basic knowledge of physics.

How to change energy waves

Science has discovered a set of basic laws for how energy waves interact with each other. When two energy waves meet, they create an "interference pattern." You can demonstrate this by putting on a pair of red glasses. The sky now appears purple, and the reason is that the blue light waves coming from the sky react with the red waves that make up the glasses. The resulting interference pattern produces a new type of energy waves, namely purple light.

The conclusion is undeniable, but it is also so simple that the human mind often refuses to acknowledge how significant it is. Everything is energy, even "solid" matter. Energy is a form of wave. You can change the properties of one energy wave by directing another wave at the first one. If the second wave has the right properties, you can transform the first one. The conclusion is that if you know how to change energy, there is no condition that you cannot change. This even holds true for physical conditions because they too are made from vibrating energy:

- Everything is made from energy that starts out with a very high vibration, namely what I have called primordial energy. This energy is first lowered to the spectrum of the identity octave. Here it begins to take on a certain form.

- The energy is then lowered to the mental octave where it takes on a more concrete or solidified form.

- It is now lowered to the emotional octave where the form becomes more concrete but still fluid.

- The final step is that the energy is lowered to the physical octave where it takes on its most dense or solid form.

The importance of this fact is that until the energy crosses the threshold to the physical octave, it is still quite fluid and easy to change. Once it has become physical, some conditions can be changed only through physical means. Before the energy becomes physical, it can be changed by directing emotional, mental or identity energy into the condition. The question now becomes how to do this.

Can we change energy?

Can we human beings change the vibration of energy waves? Are we not doing this every day? When you think, your thought has a certain content, but the driving force behind the thought is an energy wave. Where does that energy come from? According to Einstein, it comes from a higher level. Let us look at how this works through a concrete example.

One region of the world where it is possible to talk about "escalating tension" is the Middle East. People in the Middle East are very conscious of their identity as either Jews or Arabs. Their minds can be conscious because they are constantly receiving a stream of primordial energy that has been lowered to the spectrum of vibrations that make up the identity octave. When this unqualified energy enters the identity level of people's minds, it is colored or qualified by how people define themselves.

Arabs define themselves a certain way, but part of their identity is that they are different from and in opposition to Jews. The Jews also have a strong sense of identity as being different from all other people and in opposition to Arabs. Even at the highest level of people's minds, there is a conflict.

This conflict is "existential," in the sense that it is difficult to grow up as an Arab without seeing yourself in opposition to Jews and vice versa. An existential conflict is based on fear, and fear is obviously a lower vibration than love. At the highest levels of people's minds, the higher energy that keeps them conscious is qualified with a vibration of fear.

Once the energy has been colored by people's sense of identity, it descends to the mental level of the mind where it becomes the driving force for their thoughts. Because the energy has already been qualified with a pattern of conflict, there is a predefined limit to how most people think. If you identify yourself as an Arab, you see Jews as being fundamentally wrong. It now becomes very difficult to think positive thoughts about Jews. The same, of course, is true for how many Jews think about Arabs.

After the energy has been qualified at the mental level, it descends to the emotional octave where it drives people's feelings. If your psychic energy has already been qualified at the identity and mental levels, it is very difficult for you to override this at the feeling level. For most Jews, it is easy to feel love towards fellow Jews but very difficult to cultivate a feeling of love towards Palestinians or other Arabs.

The energy then leaves the emotional and enters the physical octave where it becomes the driving force behind people's actions. Based on this, is it any wonder that Arabs and Jews tend to take fear-based instead of love-based actions towards each other? Once the energy has already been qualified at the three higher levels, how can people's conscious minds override this influence?

Once in a while the international community manages to *force* Jews and Palestinians to the negotiating table (they don't do this voluntarily). People from the outside world tend to think that it should be possible for the two parties to look at the situation objectively and to negotiate rationally. What we as outsiders do not understand is that Jews and Palestinians can never be objective and rational about their relationship. They have for a very long time built up such huge reservoirs of fear-based energy between each other that it blocks any form of objectivity and rationality.

The deeper reality is that when Jews and Palestinians sit at the negotiating table, it is not human beings who are interacting. Instead, there is an interaction between two spirals or maelstroms of energy in the collective consciousness. These spirals are so intense that they will overpower any individual, and that is why peace negotiations have so far produced no significant result.

By simply observing world events, we can conclude that we human beings do have the ability to change the vibration of energy. Our minds are able to take pure, undifferentiated energy and change it to a very low vibration. The price we pay for this ability is that what we do with energy can create a spiral that can overpower our conscious minds. At the physical, conscious level we have become marionettes of the energy spirals we have created at the emotional, mental and identity levels. This is the *bad* news so let us look at the *good* news.

What the mind has created, it can uncreate

Before World War I, people in Europe had created huge spirals of energy in the identity, mental and emotional realms. Scientists say that once energy has taken on a certain vibration, it will stay in that vibration indefinitely. The energy cannot change itself and continues to accumulate. As it accumulates, it creates a kind of magnetic effect that starts to pull on people's minds.

Before the war people were quite aware of the dangers of going to war. They were able to rationally weigh the advantages against the potential consequences. For several years, there was a "balance of power" where the rational mind was able to stop nations from reacting to the build-up of fear-based energies. As the energies continued to accumulate, they eventually reached a critical mass and now even large nations were overpowered by the energy spirals. The spirals of fear and anger overpowered the rational mind and war broke out. The same mechanism prevents any real progress in negotiations between Jews and Palestinians and between many other groups of people around the world.

The good news is that what the human mind has created, it can also uncreate. When we recognize that we have the ability to qualify energy with a fear-based vibration and build negative spirals, we also see that we have the ability to undo this by using energy of a love-based vibration.

We can now go back to what scientists have discovered about energy waves. From a purely mechanical viewpoint, an energy wave of a higher vibration is more powerful than a wave of a lower vibration. If you take a wave of a low vibration and send another wave of a higher vibration at it, you can raise the vibration of the first wave. This is a matter of wave mechanics.

When we look at history, it is easy to see that we human beings have generated enormous amounts of fear-based energy. This energy starts to form spirals in the collective consciousness that can overpower people's conscious minds and cause them to make fear-based rather than rational or love-based choices. This mechanism (that we should all have been taught in kindergarten) can explain virtually all of the conflicts between human beings, from family quarrels to world-wide wars.

As we have the ability to generate fear-based energy, we also have the ability to use love-based energy and build positive spirals. We know that love-based energy can transform fear-based energy. We know that people have generated enormous spirals of fear-based energy. Because love-based energy is more powerful, a small amount of love-based energy can transform a large amount of fear-based energy. Even though a large number of people generate fear-based energy, a much smaller number of people generating love-based energy can counter-act the build-up of fear-based energy.

This makes it entirely feasible that a small number of people dedicated to producing and releasing love-based energy can have a decisive impact on world events. If you can use love-based energy to stop the build-up of fear-based energy spirals, you can have a decisive impact on what people do at the physical level. Accepting this and acting upon it is not a matter of wishful thinking. It is a matter of taking a look at scientific findings and accepting the logical conclusions.

We now see that we human beings – in principle – have the ability to use love-based energy to transform fear-based energy. Next we need to look at practical ways of doing this so that our efforts have the greatest possible effect.

2 | HOW TO TRANSFORM FEAR-BASED ENERGY

The Holy Grail of materialistic science has been objectivity. Since materialists started trying to distance science from religion, they have claimed that any belief in beings beyond the material universe is superstition. They say the belief in spiritual beings is a product of the human mind and its subjectivity. Materialists have tried to take all influence of the mind out of science by inventing instruments and methods that are completely materialistic. They have said that only what can be measured by such instruments has any reality. What materialists refuse to acknowledge is that all of their claims have now been invalidated by scientific discoveries.

The basic claim of materialists is that it is possible for a scientist to be a neutral observer. A scientist can be separated from the phenomenon he or she is observing so that the mind of the scientist has no influence on the outcome of the experiment. As far back as the 1930s, quantum physicists discovered that at the level of subatomic particles there is no such thing as a neutral observer.

At the deepest level of matter, everything is in a fundamental way interconnected. When a scientist studies a subatomic phenomenon, his or her mind becomes part of the "measurement situation." The scientist is not observing something that takes place independently of the mind. The mind of the scientist becomes part of the process and has a direct influence on the outcome of the experiment. The scientist is actually a co-creator of the observed phenomenon rather than an outside observer.

This raises a couple of questions that have a direct influence on the topic of how we can help change the world. The subatomic world is the most subtle level of the material world. It is the border between the world of matter particles and a realm of pure energy. It is where pure energy is lowered in vibration so it takes on the form of matter particles. This means subatomic phenomena come into being before any of the macroscopic phenomena we can observe with our senses. Subatomic phenomena are the level of cause and the matter "things" we can see are the level of effect. As we have said before, *effect* cannot produce *cause*—it is the other way around.

It has been proven that the human mind can interact with the subatomic world, a level that came into existence a very long time before the gray matter between our ears. If our consciousness was the exclusive product of material processes in our brains, how can we explain that our minds can interact with a level of the world that came into existence about 15 billion years before our physical brains?

If our minds are entirely material phenomena, how do we explain that they can shape phenomena in the subatomic world? Are we to conclude that the minds that are produced by the gross matter of our brains can control the far subtler "matter" at the subatomic level? The only other logical possibility is to propose that there must be a form of consciousness present at the subatomic level. Our minds can interact with this primordial consciousness and it is through this process that we can influence the formation of subatomic phenomena.

This is anathema to materialists, but given that there is no other logical explanation, some scientists have begun to adapt the motto of Sherlock Holmes: "When you have eliminated the impossible, whatever remains, however improbable, must be the truth." These scientists have begun to realize that the universe is not like the machine proposed by materialists but more like a giant, undivided mind. The universe is one mind and we are part of it.

Where do we get love-based energy?

The possibility that there is a form of consciousness that underlies all material phenomena is the foundation for our ability to change the world. Einstein proved that the world is created from energy that has been reduced in vibration from a very high state to a much lower spectrum. The world is made from a stream of high-frequency energy that flows into the spectrum where our physical bodies and our planet exist.

This energy does not simply stream into our spectrum; it also takes on specific forms, from subatomic particles to solar systems and pineapples. What makes the undifferentiated energy take on specific forms?

Materialists claim all of the complex phenomena we see are the result of an unconscious and random process, but they fail to explain how this process could work. Their attempts at an explanation require as much faith in the unexplained as the doctrines of medieval theologians. A far more logical explanation is that energy takes on form by being directed through the consciousness of self-aware beings.

This raises a logical question. Given that human beings (or at least human bodies) came into existence long after the Big Bang, we could not have created the physical universe. The explanation is that the universe was given the form it has by a number of beings who are self-aware but whose minds exist in a higher energy spectrum than the physical world. These beings existed before the material world and they directed the flow of undifferentiated energy, causing it to flow into the matrices that define all physical phenomena.

These spiritual beings are still there, and they are still sending energy into our world. Science says that energy can neither be created nor destroyed. As Einstein's equation proves, this cannot be an absolute truth. Energy must come from a realm that is far beyond the material spectrum. What we call material energy is "created" when primordial energy is lowered in vibration. According to quantum physics, our minds have the potential to be part of this process.

Scientists are correct in the sense that we human beings cannot create or destroy energy. Our minds can change the vibration of energy, but we cannot create the energy. The conclusion is that our minds can receive energy from a higher realm, energy that has been lowered into our spectrum by beings who have a higher level of consciousness than we do. Our minds can be open doors for love-based energy to stream into this world. Once the energy has crossed the border into our spectrum, we can either direct it as love-based energy or we can reduce its vibration so it becomes fear-based energy.

As we have discussed, all material phenomena and all phenomena in society have a basis in vibrating energy. Many phenomena in this world can be directly linked to the accumulation of lower or fear-based energies. The only way to change the world is to use higher or love-based energies to transform the lower energies. It stands to reason that since we can generate fear-based energy, we can also become open doors for love-based energy. Bringing more love-based energy into the world is the only way to remove the huge spirals of fear-based energy that have been built over time.

Where must love-based energy come from? It must come from self-aware beings in a higher realm. The question now becomes whether these beings will give us this energy indiscriminately or whether they make an evaluation based on our state of consciousness?

Energy is the driving force behind all material phenomena. It is often said that if you have enough money, you can buy anything you want. The real "currency" in the world is energy. If you have enough energy, you can *do* anything you want.

Now take a look at human behavior. Imagine that the most selfish people in the world received lots of creative energy. They might use it to set themselves up as dictators who could enslave other people. Would intelligent beings in a higher realm want to give energy to such people? Or would they rather give it to people who could keep it at the level of love and use it to raise up all life?

How energy runs the world

We can now begin to see how the world truly works. A very long time ago a group of self-aware beings in a higher realm created the material universe. They did so by using the powers of their minds. They had the ability to receive creative energy from an even higher realm and they then lowered it to the spectrum that makes up our world. These beings formed certain thought matrices in their minds and they projected them upon the undifferentiated energy. This caused the energy to take on the form of subatomic particles, then atoms, then molecules and then stars, planets and galaxies.

One of the last steps in the creative process was the creation of self-aware beings who would go into the newly created world in order to experience and co-create the world from the inside. I know this sketchy description does not explain everything so I go into greater depth in other books (See *The Power of Self* and *Cosmology of Evil*). I will not go into more detail here because it would take us too far from the topic of how we can help change the world.

What I *will* explain here is the question of why the world was created. The deeper reality is that the material universe is a kind of educational institution. It is created in order to teach us how to develop and use the creative potential of our minds.

We create by using energy. We give this energy specific form by allowing it to stream through our minds. The matrices we hold in our minds will determine what form the energies take on. We start out with a fairly limited level of self-awareness, and in that state we receive limited creative energies from the beings in the higher realm. As we expand our self-awareness, we have the potential to move beyond all selfishness and realize what scientists have now proven, namely that the world is one, interconnected whole. If we harm other people, we are also harming ourselves. The best way to raise up ourselves is to work for raising the whole by releasing love-based energy. As we transcend selfishness, we will receive more creative energy and can have a greater impact on the world.

Most religions have the concept that in the past, human beings lived in a kind of paradise. We have since "fallen" into the state we see today where there is old age, disease, limitations, suffering and conflict. This idea of a lost paradise is meant to symbolize that most people on earth have descended

2 | How to Transform Fear-Based Energy

into a selfish state of consciousness. In this state, they can no longer receive very much creative energy from a higher realm. The effect of this is profound.

The driving force in the world is energy. The world was originally created by beings in a higher realm who allowed a certain amount of energy to be lowered to our spectrum. This was our initial gift of creative energy. Jesus gave a profound parable about three servants who received different amounts of talents from their master. Two of them multiplied their talents while one buried them in the ground. The first two received more in return whereas the third one received nothing more. This symbolizes that after the initial amount of energy, the world can receive more energy only when we make wise use of what we have. The world can receive additional energy only through the minds of people in embodiment.

If we use energies selfishly, we cut ourselves off from receiving more energy from above. This explains why there is lack and suffering in the word. There is not enough love-based, creative energy in our frequency spectrum to provide physical abundance for all of the people living on earth. This is not because some angry God in the sky wants to punish us. It is because we have chosen to cut ourselves off from the flow of creative energy. We have turned our world into a closed system, meaning a system that is receiving less energy from beyond itself. A basic natural law, which scientists calls the second law of thermodynamics, states that a closed system will gradually self-destruct.

When there is only a certain amount of creative energy available in the world, it is inevitable that there will be lack. The lack of material resources is a symbol for the lack of creative energy. The inevitable result is that people must compete with each other for a limited amount of energy, which can only lead to ongoing conflict and struggle. Basically all of the conflicts between human beings have their roots in this struggle over a limited amount of creative energy. No matter what we do in life, we need energy in order to do it. We have two ways of getting energy:

- We can get it from the finite pool of energy that has already been lowered into our spectrum.

- We can get it from the unlimited pool of energy in a higher realm.

Once energy has been lowered into our spectrum, we human beings can use it in two ways:

- We can use it selflessly, which keeps it at a higher vibration where it has more creative power.

- We can use it in selfish ways, which lowers its vibration and reduces its creative power.

History shows us how we have so often used energy in selfish ways and thereby lowered it to the fear-based spectrum. This fear-based energy has less creative power than love-based energy. The more fear-based energy we generate, the more we reduce our creative potential, meaning we intensify the struggle for a limited amount or energy.

This can become a downward spiral that is self-reinforcing. As we have less energy, we must take it from each other. This generates more conflict, which generates even more fear-based energy. There is only one way to reverse the trend and that is to bring more love-based energy. Love-based energy can break the vicious circle and give people the opportunity to break out of selfish patterns.

The problem is that love-based energy can be brought into the world only through the minds of people who have been willing to raise their consciousness above selfishness. Once you have done this, even if not completely, you can receive more energy from above. You can also make use of tools for directly and consciously invoking love-based energy and using it to transform fear-based energy. This is how a few people can have a decisive impact on the evolution in society.

We now see the key that can allow a relatively small number of spiritually minded people to have a decisive impact on the world. The essential task is to bring more love-based energy into the material spectrum. We can do this through our minds, but we cannot produce the energy by ourselves. We must receive it from self-aware beings in a realm of higher vibrations, and that means we need to learn how to work with these beings.

Why we do not know about beings in a higher realm

Most of us were brought up in a war-zone, caught in a battle between scientific materialism and traditional religion, often Christianity. Both of these thought systems portray us as essentially powerless beings who are cut off from beings in a higher realm.

Materialism says there is nothing beyond the material world and that believing in the traditional God makes you a superstitious fool. Traditional religion says there *is* a world beyond the material, but we are personally cut off from it. The higher world is populated by an angry God who watches everything we do and will condemn us to an eternity in hell if we do not follow the commands of the religion here on earth. There may be a few angels up there as well, but definitely no beings we can relate to personally. The favors of the angry God can only be secured by obeying the priesthood here on earth.

The hidden mechanism behind both systems is that there is a certain group of beings who want to keep us disempowered. Elitism is the missing link in our ability to make sense of history. There has always been a power elite of beings who want to pacify the general population so they can be controlled. Some power elite groups use religion in order to control us, others use political systems and still others use scientific materialism.

The leaders of the power elite want to pacify those of us who have a higher level of awareness and have the potential to bring something from a higher realm that will challenge their control over the earth. I will not go into great detail about the power elite in this book because I have already described the origin and methods of the power elite in the book *Cosmology of Evil*.

I only want to mention the power elite as the reason we were not brought up with the knowledge that there are beings in a higher realm who are ready to help us. The members of the power elite do not want us to receive the clearer vision and the energy that will empower us to overthrow the power elite through peaceful means. Who are the higher beings that can give us the energy and the instructions we need in order to change the world?

Why the ascended masters are not saviors

In order to avoid referring to them as "beings in a higher realm," I would like to name them "ascended masters." The name signifies that these beings have attained the ultimate self-mastery that comes from transcending all selfishness. They have realized the underlying reality that all life is one, meaning that the only way to raise up yourself is to raise up all life. The ascended masters are serving selflessly and some of them have taken on the task of helping us rise above the level of selfishness.

The name also signifies that some of the ascended masters have been in embodiment on earth as we are now. They have gone through the same process we are going through and they know first-hand the immense challenges we face on a planet as dense as the earth. Obviously, not all members of the ascended masters have ascended from this planet. Some have ascended from other planets in the material universe while others ascended in previous spheres. These spheres existed before our world was created. For a deeper explanation of this process, see *Cosmology of Evil* or *The Power of Self*.

The ascended masters are nothing like the angry God in the sky, nor are they like the traditional concept of angels who flutter around in a remote realm. The ascended masters are very much present with us—if we allow them to be part of our lives. They are selflessly working to fulfill the task they have taken on, namely to raise the earth beyond the level of selfishness so that this beautiful planet can once again be free from fear-based energies.

The ascended masters have access to unlimited amounts of love-based energy. They could instantly release so much energy that it would consume all of the fear-based energy that surrounds the planet like a dark cloud. Because the earth is an educational institution for us who are in embodiment, the ascended masters do not have the authority to remove all darkness from earth. They cannot release energy directly into the physical spectrum but must do so through our minds. They can release love-based energy through us only to the extent that we have raised ourselves beyond selfishness so we will not misuse the energy. Traditional religions often portray us as powerless to work out our "salvation." Instead, it is claimed that an external savior will come and take us to heaven. The reality is that the only "saviors" that will ever come to this planet are the ascended masters. They will not save us, but they will give us the knowledge and the energy that will empower us to raise our consciousness beyond selfishness and thereby qualify for the ascension to the spiritual realm. The salvation of ourselves and of the planet is truly a do-it-yourself project.

The true meaning of salvation is that we permanently ascend to the spiritual realm and do not have to come back into embodiment on earth. The ascended masters have already gone through that process and that is why they are the best possible guides for us. The forces who work against our ascension (because they want to keep us under their control) will do anything in their power to keep us from knowing about ascended masters or accepting their intercession. They especially want to prevent us from accepting our rightful role in relation to the ascended masters.

The ascended masters and us

When you first hear about ascended masters, it is very easy to take the image of God perpetuated by traditional religions and apply it to the masters. This is non-constructive because it prevents us from accepting our rightful role here on earth. It causes us to see the masters as beings who exist in some remote heaven world. It causes us to see ourselves as being cut off from the masters.

The deeper reality is that everything is united and that the link is consciousness. Everything is created out of consciousness, meaning that the material universe is created by the ascended masters and they created it out of their own minds. We too are extensions of the minds of the ascended masters.

The entire idea that we could be separated from the beings who are our source is the extreme outcome of the consciousness of selfishness.

This state of mind causes us to see ourselves as separate beings. We are separated from our source, which means we cannot receive directions or energy from a higher realm. We are separated from each other, and this is what makes conflict between people possible. We are separated from the planet on which we live, and this is what causes us to create environmental problems.

When we begin to rise above this illusion of separation, we see that each of us is connected to an ascended master. This master serves as our personal guide. The master has only one concern, namely to help us rise above the separate state of mind. The master is nothing like the angry and judgmental God who seeks to make us feel bad for what we have done or not done. Instead, the master only looks forward and seeks to help us rise above any and all aspects of selfishness.

The master will help us see how we keep ourselves trapped in a lower state of mind by clinging to illusions and old habit patterns. This may be somewhat shocking to our egos, but it is ultimately liberating. Our personal master is always seeking to awaken us and never uses fear, guilt or shame in order to do so. The master is in a permanent love-based state of mind and simply cannot use fear-based means.

Why have you grown up without any awareness of ascended masters? Part of the explanation is the power elite groups that have defined the dominant thought systems on earth. They do not want us to know who we really are and what our creative potential is. Another part of the explanation is that matter on earth is still so dense that it is not easy to experience the ascended masters directly. Our minds function somewhat like radio receivers. As a radio can be tuned to different stations, so can our minds. Through a combination of the power elite and the density of matter, we have been brought up to attune our minds to the material frequency spectrum. We all have the potential to free ourselves from this programming and learn how to tune our minds to the ascended masters. Taking your mind away from a focus on the material octave and tuning in to the ascended masters in the spiritual realm is the real goal of all forms of spiritual growth. It is by doing this that we can fulfill the purpose for which we volunteered to come to this planet.

The authority we have on earth

As we begin to explore and expand our sense of being connected to our personal master, we can come to an even deeper realization. We are not actually separate beings who are connected to a remote master up there in heaven. Everything is created from consciousness and you are an extension of the mind of an ascended master. This can eventually help us develop a sense of oneness with one or more ascended masters.

Even if it takes a while for you to develop this oneness, it is still important to understand that oneness is the underlying reality. This helps us accept that we have a right to be here on earth. We have a right to be "spiritual but not religious." We have a right to follow a different path than most people. First of all, we have a right to reach for a higher state of consciousness and express that state of consciousness. We have a right to become open doors for the direction and the energy coming from the ascended masters and thereby pull up the collective consciousness.

We can then begin to accept how the Law of Free Will works. This law says that the people who are in physical embodiment have the ultimate authority for what kind of conditions exist on earth. The level of limitations, conflict and suffering is directly linked to the balance between love-based and fear-based energy. The many limitations seen on this earth are the direct result of the fact that this planet is dominated by fear-based energies.

The earth is in some ways still in a self-reinforcing downward spiral, such as seen in the Middle East. This is why most people see themselves as separate beings and are not open to receiving directions and love-based energy from the ascended masters. In fact, most people deny or ridicule the idea of ascended masters.

One might say that this proves most people still want to experience limitations and suffering and they should be allowed to do so. The problem with this view is that most people on earth do not have the vision that there is an alternative to present conditions. If you read books about the end of the Soviet Union, you will find that there was a pivotal moment when Boris Yeltsin visited the United States. He made an unscheduled stop at a normal grocery store and while seeing the abundance of goods on the shelves, he realized that the communist system had been upheld only because the people inside were ignorant about how life was outside the system. If people truly *know* better, most of them will *do* better.

The Law of Free Will allows even a few beings in embodiment to change the equation for the entire planet. We who are willing to open our hearts and minds to the ascended masters can become forerunners for a planetary shift. We can bring in so much love-based energy that more and more people start to awaken from their selfishness and begin to see that there is an alternative to the present state of conflict and struggle.

This awakening process has been going on for some time now, but it still has not reached the critical mass that awakens the majority. That is why the ascended masters have taken various steps to work with the people who have already started to awaken or who are willing to become part of this process. It is to this end that the ascended masters have sponsored this book, many other teachings and the tools that will be presented in coming chapters.

3 | YOUR LIFE'S PURPOSE

The ascended masters teach that the material world is an educational institution. It is designed to help us start out with a localized sense of self and then gradually expand it until we rise above selfishness. From this perspective, all human beings are in the process of raising their awareness and expanding their sense of self. There are two ways to approach this process: aware and unaware. Normally, we start out being unaware of the process and how it works. Over a long period of time (meaning many embodiments or lifetimes on earth) we evolve to becoming more aware of the process.

The masters say there are many planets in the material universe with self-aware beings. Most of these planets have already evolved to a higher level than earth, meaning you do not find war and conflict on them. The people on these planets have raised the individual and collective consciousness to a level where war is unthinkable. This obviously is not the case on earth and the reason is that most people have not risen above the level of selfishness.

According to the masters, an entire planet can go into a self-reinforcing downward spiral that can end with the destruction of the planet or the eradication of all higher life forms on it. In the distant past, the earth had entered such a spiral. In order to prevent its destruction, the ascended masters allowed lifestreams from other planets to embody on earth and this has now turned things around.

If you are open to the ideas presented in this book, it is likely that you were among the lifestreams who volunteered to embody on earth in order to help raise this planet. It is also possible you were one of the lifestreams that started out on earth and you have now started to become aware of how the process of life works. You have started to realize that you are not on this planet only for your own sake. If the ideas in this book resonate with you, it is because helping to raise the planet is part of why you are in embodiment in this lifetime. The masters teach that before the more aware lifestreams come into a given embodiment, they always meet with a group of ascended masters. The purpose is to formulate a plan for your coming embodiment. We might call it a life plan or a Divine plan.

This plan is made from a much higher level of awareness than you have once you are inside a dense physical body and outer mind. It incorporates many aspects, including what you personally need to learn or overcome in order to make maximum progress on your individual path towards the ascension. It also incorporates what you can do to help raise the earth. This can range from raising your individual consciousness to doing specific things in society. Because the earth is so dense, it is almost impossible to remember all aspects of your Divine plan once you are inside the body. It is important to know this because your Divine plan is not something that is forced upon you by an angry God. The ascended masters who guide you are only trying to help you, and you are the one who has the final say regarding all aspects of your Divine plan. The masters force nothing upon you. You choose everything yourself.

The problem is that you choose based on the wider awareness you have before coming into a dense body on this dense planet. You will lose this wider perspective once you are in the body, and that means you have no conscious memory of your Divine plan. It also means your outer mind can rebel against certain aspects of the plan that you chose. Many spiritual people have to go through a period of struggling with themselves before they gain the clarity and acceptance of what they truly want to do in life. Most spiritual people have some sense that they have a purpose or mission, but we are often unclear about the details. Why do we have this lack of vision? It is because the energies of our physical bodies and the energies on the planet are so dense that they obscure our vision. These energies form a veil (energy veil is the deeper meaning of evil) that traps us in a limited vision.

What can you do to gain a clearer perspective on your Divine plan? You can invoke love-based energy in order to transform some of the fear-based energy that limits your vision. The tools presented in this book will not only have an impact on the world. Using them will also have an impact on your own path by making you gradually more aware of your Divine plan. As you gain a clearer vision of what you chose from a higher perspective, it will become easier for you to see what to do and to accept that this is what you truly want to do. This is a win for both you and the planet.

What is in your Divine plan?

All societies on earth program their members to live according to the norms of their society. This is not necessarily bad or evil; it is simply how life works. Of course, no society on earth currently has norms that make it easy for spiritual people to fulfill their Divine plans.

You are a unique individual. Because you are more spiritually aware than most people in your environment, you are not in embodiment in order to conform to the norms of your society. In order to fulfill your Divine plan, you will most likely have to go beyond these norms. It may even be part of your Divine plan to challenge these norms. After all, how can a society grow unless some people challenge the norms that keep people trapped in old patterns? For example, how can a society escape patterns of violence unless some people refuse to react through fear?

Your Divine plan is not something that is set in stone. The ascended masters know from direct experience how difficult it is to be in embodiment on a planet as dense as this one. There is plenty of room in your Divine plan for making your own choices and for making what seems like mistakes. As spiritual people become more aware of their Divine plans, they often find that they have always followed their plan in the big decisions in life. When it comes to the details, we have often done things that we might later regret, but in the big decisions, we have had enough attunement to know what to do. We may not always have been aware of why it was important to do something, such as enter a relationship or change jobs, but we have had a sense that this was what we had to do and we have done it.

As you use the tools in this book, this clarity will increase until you begin to see why you needed to do what you did and what you will do in the future. This will happen in part as a result of you learning to invoke love-based energy, or spiritual light. What currently blocks the vision of your Divine plan is fear-based energy. Is it not obvious that as you begin to invoke love-based energy, the lower energies will be cleared away and your vision will improve? Let us briefly look at some examples of what might be in your Divine plan and how invoking light can help you fulfill your life's purpose:

- You may have karma with certain people from past lives. As an opportunity to balance it, you have relationships with them in this life as parents, siblings, spouses, people at work etcetera. Invoking light helps you transmute the karma much more quickly and makes it easier for you and others to break out of old patterns.

- You may have volunteered to help certain people grow personally or spiritually by having relationships with them. Invoking light on their behalf can help them more quickly rise above their issues.

- You may have volunteered to help certain people with a very difficult psychology, even abusive tendencies. You may have volunteered to embody in a close relationship with such a person even though there is a risk the person will abuse you. You will have done this in order to give the person an opportunity to either rise above the pattern or be judged by his or her actions and thus lose the opportunity to hurt others. Invoking light can heal both yourself and the other person, even clear the collective consciousness.

- You may have volunteered to help many people rise above a particular problem, such as disease, substance abuse, a difficult childhood or many other problems. It was not your karma that made it necessary to experience such difficult situations. You did it with the goal of helping others. In order to fulfill that goal, you have to know what they are going through. By rising above such problems, you carve a trail in the collective consciousness. By your example, you inspire others to rise above the same issue. Invoking light can protect and heal you. It can heal other people and cut them free from negative patterns. It can also bring about a judgment of other people or any dark forces using them. This can cause these people or the dark forces to be removed from the earth, lightening the burden of fear-based energy.

• You may be part of a new trend that will take society forward. This can be virtually anything from a new way to raise or teach children or bringing greater awareness about a specific problem. All spiritual people are helping bring society towards a recognition of the spiritual side of life and how it can help us solve problems that otherwise seem to have no solution. It can also be many other activities. Invoking light is extremely efficient for clearing the collective consciousness so that people can break free of old destructive patterns and embrace a new approach.

• You may have the capacity to bring forth a new idea or invention in a specific area of life. This can be anything from writing books, engaging in politics on some level, going into business, working as a scientist or making an invention. Invoking light will help you gain a more clear vision of what you are meant to bring forth. It will also help bring the idea down to the physical level and clear the way for it being accepted by others.

- You may have volunteered to hold a kind of spiritual balance for specific other people, your nation or the planet as a whole. Invoking light is almost the only way to have maximum impact on holding this balance. It is the fastest way for you to help balance planetary karma and clear the way for a new and better age.

- You may have volunteered to help raise people's awareness of the spiritual side of life, either through a specific religion or spiritual philosophy, through science or through the teachings of the ascended masters. Invoking light provides a driving force that helps you know what to do and gives you the momentum to break through the resistance.

It is not the intention here to say that you should only sit at home and invoke light. If it is in your Divine plan to go out and do something for other people or society, you clearly should do so. If you do not currently have a clear vision of what is in your Divine plan, the most likely solution is that your vision is being blocked by fear-based energy either in your own consciousness or in the collective consciousness.

Using appropriate tools to invoke light can greatly enhance your vision. Even when you have a clear vision, no matter what you are here to accomplish in this lifetime, invoking light can help you become more successful in your endeavors. It can be the difference between breaking through and getting things done or being held back by the inevitable opposition from the fear-based energies that hang over the planet.

How invoking light helps your Divine plan

The material universe has four distinct levels, and that means your Divine plan needs to be manifest in four stages. You have a blueprint of your Divine plan at the identity level, but it needs to be brought into the mental, then the emotional and then the physical in order for you to see manifest results. The descent of your Divine blueprint to the next level can be blocked by fear-based energy in any of the four levels of your mind, your energy field. It can also be blocked by energies in the collective consciousness.

By invoking light from the ascended masters, you can consume the fear-based energy accumulated at all four levels of your personal energy field. You can also invoke love-based energy to provide the driving force for the manifestation of your Divine plan. Doing this will give you a clearer vision of your plan and give you the creative energy to implement your vision.

The fulfillment of your Divine plan rarely depends on you alone. It often involves other people. These people can also be blocked by fear-based energy at the four levels of their minds. Invoking light will also help to purify other people.

Your Divine plan may be aimed at bringing change to some area of society. There will be an accumulation of fear-based energy in the four levels of the collective consciousness or planetary energy field. This can also be cleared by invoking light.

The ascended masters recommend that each of us becomes an expert in a specific field. This does not mean we have to have a formal education or work in the field. It means we pick a topic that is dear to our hearts and then we educate ourselves in the dynamics involved with the topic. Even if we do not physically do anything within the field, our knowledge forms the basis for our making more precise calls for the consuming of the energies that block change.

As an example, suppose you feel a strong concern for the economy. You would read books about the topic until you had a good understanding. You could then use this knowledge to call forth spiritual light and direct it into the conditions that you see are blocking creative change. You may never work directly in the field of the economy, but your calls can help other people whose Divine plans do involve them working in the field. They may not be open to the ascended masters so by you making the calls, you can call their Divine plans into physical manifestation. You can have a positive impact on the economy without working in the field at the physical level.

Your Divine plan was made in cooperation with the ascended masters that work with you personally. You will not be successful in fulfilling your Divine plan by working with human power alone. Bringing the ascended masters into your life, both as guides and as the source of creative energy, is essential to your success. Using the tools given by the ascended masters is the most successful way to invoke their presence and energy.

4 | A CLOSER LOOK AT ASCENDED MASTERS

You cannot prove that ascended masters exist by using traditional arguments. It is by no means the intent of this book to talk you into believing anything you don't want to believe. If it is in your Divine plan to find and make use of the teachings of the ascended masters, what you have read in this book will resonate with something in the core of your being. You will have an inner, intuitive sense that there is something here for you. The reason is that you have already established some inner, mystical, intuitive connection to the ascended masters in past lifetimes.

The important task for you is not to find or follow an outer teaching, organization, guru or ritual. The important task is to expand and clarify the inner connection you already have with the masters and your higher self. If the teachings and tools presented in the books in this series can help you do this, by all means make use of them. If not, please seek other teachings about ascended masters and apply them until your vision is clarified and you know from within what is your mission on earth.

There are many ascended masters and they have different functions. Their names may sound alien based on the culture you grew up in, but often you will have a sense that a certain name stirs something inside you or resonates with your own being. The explanation is that you have an inner connection to that master.

The purpose of this chapter is to give you an overview of how ascended masters are organized and what their roles are for this planet. You will also find short descriptions of some of the masters who work most closely with earth. If none of the masters mentioned here resonates with you, please seek out other descriptions until you find your personal master. You will find descriptions of the masters and messages from many ascended masters on the website *www.ascendedmasterligt.com*

How the ascended masters are organized

Although you have one master who is your personal master, you will not invoke the light of only that master. In order to have the greatest impact on changing the world, you will invoke light of different masters for different purposes. There are four main categories of ascended masters:

- **The Elohim.** The material world is created from energy, but not just one type of energy. There are seven creative energies, also called the seven spiritual rays. Each ray has certain qualities and it is by combining these creative characteristics that the physical universe was created. The beings who created the earth belong to the elohimic level, meaning they have the creative power to create a structure as complex as a solar system and a planet. There are seven Elohim, one for each ray, and each Elohim has a female counterpart. The Elohim still hold the original, unpolluted blueprint for planet earth. You invoke the Elohim in order to bring the creative energy and the vision that can restore the original blueprint.

- **The Archangels.** Angels and Archangels serve in a variety of capacities. An Archangel serves on a specific spiritual ray but whereas the Elohim serve to create a planet, the Archangels serve to uphold it and to help it grow. The Archangels also bring the light to counteract the specific forms of fear-based energy that block change on earth. The dark forces that exist on earth are best stopped by invoking the Archangels.

- **The Chohans.** For each ray there is one master who serves as the main teacher, helping us internalize and use the qualities of the ray. There are also other masters who serve on a given ray. You invoke the Chohan in order to learn how to use a ray and in order to awaken others.

- **Other masters.** There are many masters who serve on more than one ray or who serve a more broad office. For example, Mother Mary is the representative of the Divine Mother Flame for earth. Jesus holds the Office of Planetary Savior. Gautama Buddha holds the Office of the Lord of the World. Lord Maitreya holds the Office of Planetary Teacher. Saint Germain holds the Office of the Age of Aquarius, the cycle our planet will be going through over the next 2,000 years. There are also masters who are at an even higher level than the Elohim, and they are called cosmic beings. One example is Shiva who is very powerful for consuming illusions and lower energies. The Great Divine Director can obviously help you gain a clearer vision and sense of direction concerning your Divine plan. Surya can help you bring balance. Alpha and Omega are the highest representatives of God that we know of, and they represent the original polarity of the expanding and contracting forces of creation.

A short description of the spiritual rays

This is not meant to be a complete description of the spiritual rays and their qualities. You can find more information in some of the other books and on *www.transcendencetoolbox.com*. The purpose of this description is to give you a feel for the rays and how they relate to changing the world.

It was the energies of the seven rays that was used to create the earth in its pure form. The planet is currently far below the original blueprint, and this has happened because people in embodiment have misused and perverted the spiritual rays. Nothing can be created without the energies of the spiritual rays, but it is possible to create lower forms by using a fear-based perversion of the rays. All imperfect and impure manifestations you see on earth are created through a perversion of one or several of the spiritual rays. As we have seen, the key to transforming lower energies is to invoke higher energies. There is no condition on earth that cannot be transformed by invoking the love-based energies of one or several spiritual rays. A particular form of lower energy is best transformed by invoking the pure form of that energy.

4 | A Closer Look at Ascended Masters

First Ray

The color of the light is electric blue and the creative qualities are will and power. In order to bring forth anything, you need the will to create and a certain momentum to carry it through to manifestation. Obviously, the earth has many perversions of the first ray where people have an impure will and are misusing power, often through the belief that the ends can justify the means. The First Ray is closely linked to government and any position of power.

- The Elohim of the First Ray is Hercules. You invoke his energy in order to restore the vision and blueprint for how organizations or governments can function at their highest level.

- The Archangel is Michael. On the personal level you invoke Archangel Michael for spiritual protection. On the planetary level, you invoke him for consuming all abuses of power and for binding the dark forces that control people in power. People who abuse power, such as dictators, are often controlled by dark beings in the emotional realm and Archangel Michael can bind or consume such beings.

- The Chohan is Master MORE and you invoke him for learning how to use power in a balanced manner. You also invoke him for helping people learn the highest use of power in government, organizations and any form of leadership.

You invoke the energies of the First Ray in order to bring change into any area of society that deals with government, leadership and leadership training, money and finance and any type of large organization, including the military. The corresponding chakra is the Throat Chakra.

Second Ray

The color of the light is golden yellow and the creative qualities are wisdom, understanding and illumination. This relates especially to evaluating the result of your creative efforts and making adjustments. When you are in the process of learning how to master your creative abilities, you start out by using the will and power of the First Ray to experiment. You then evaluate the outcome by using the Second Ray and making adjustments before your next effort.

One of the primary perversions of the Second Ray seen on earth is the belief that a particular system, such as Christianity, scientific materialism or communism, can tell us how the world is supposed to work. We then refuse to compare our results to reality and make adjustments. We think that if we continue applying the system long enough, the world will comply. Obviously, the Second Ray is closely linked to education and any form of intellectual endeavor.

- The Elohim of the Second Ray is Apollo and you invoke his energy to restore the vision of how no system is enough in itself and how we can create a culture of being willing to learn from our experiments.

- The Archangel is Jophiel and you invoke him in order to break up established systems of thought and bind the dark forces that seek to keep people's minds trapped in limited patterns.

- The Chohan is Master Lanto and you invoke him to bring change and vision into any kind of education.

You invoke the energies of the Second Ray in order to bring change into any area of society that deals with education, science and intellectual activities. The corresponding chakra is the Crown Chakra.

Third Ray

The color of the light is pink and the creative qualities are love, balance and the willingness to transcend. Love is a great challenge on earth because it has been so perverted. Most of what people call love is not the unconditional Divine love but a human possessive love.

The primary perversion of love on earth is the sense of ownership towards both things and people. This causes people to want to stop growth and maintain a certain state indefinitely. True love gives you the love for something that is more than what you have now, making you willing to flow with the creative energies in constant self-transcendence.

- The Elohim of the Third Ray is Heros and you invoke his energy for any creative expression, such as art or music.

- The Archangel is Chamuel and you invoke him in order to break up established patterns of relationships and in order to bind or consume all forces of anti-love.

- The Chohan is Paul the Venetian and you invoke him in order to learn how to be creative in art, music and relationships. He will also teach you how to discern between unreality and reality.

You invoke the energies of the Third Ray in order to bring change into any area of society that deals with art, music, relationships and families. The corresponding chakra is the Heart Chakra.

Fourth Ray

The color of the light is white and the creative qualities are purity and acceleration. The white light of the Fourth Ray is also called the Mother Light and the corresponding chakra is the base chakra that is located near the sexual organs. Obviously, one of the primary perversions of the Fourth Ray on earth is any kind of sexual perversion, including advertising. Discipline is also a quality of the Fourth Ray and it has been perverted into two opposite polarities, either strict discipline that recognizes no inner guidance or the opposite that recognizes no restrictions.

- The Elohim of the Fourth Ray is Purity and his female consort Astrea. You invoke their energy to restore purity in any activity or condition. Invoking the energy of Astrea is extremely efficient for cutting yourself or others free from old patterns, fear-based energies and dark forces, including forces that cause addictions. Astrea will also consume these conditions on the collective level.

- The Archangel is Gabriel and you invoke him in order to consume all conditions that keep people trapped in a misuse of the Mother Light through the

4 | A Closer Look at Ascended Masters

base chakra, such as sex addiction, pornography and any kind of addiction.

- The Chohan is Serapis Bey and you invoke him to learn the correct and balanced use of the Mother Light.

You invoke the energies of the Fourth Ray in order to bring change into architecture, the military, planning at higher levels, city planning, mathematics and related fields. The corresponding chakra is the Base Chakra.

Fifth Ray

The color of the light is emerald green and the creative qualities are vision and truth. One of the major problems on earth is that people's vision of what is possible has been so restricted. For example, many people think that a lack of natural resources is both "natural" and inevitable. In reality, the resources available in the physical octave can be increased by bringing more creative energy into this octave. This can happen only through the minds of the people in embodiment.

If our vision is limited, we cannot serve as open doors. This makes it possible that the inhabitants of a planet can have such a limited vision that it becomes a self-fulfilling prophecy. People are so convinced that resources are limited that they refuse to open their minds to creative energies. This will limit the resources and as they are used up, people become more set in a limited vision, restricting the creative flow even more.

- The Elohim of the Fifth Ray is Cyclopea and you invoke his energy to restore vision to the healing arts, communication and discovery of new truths.

- The Archangel is Raphael and you invoke him in order to break up a limited vision and bring healing energies.

- The Chohan is Hilarion and you invoke him to bring change and vision into the healing arts, complex technology, communications and media, music and the interface between science and religion.

You invoke the energies of the Fifth Ray in order to restore what can be called the immaculate vision or immaculate concept. This involves both the vision of how the earth was in its pure state but also a vision of how we are meant to build on that foundation and manifest a golden age on earth. The corresponding chakra is the Third Eye Chakra.

Sixth Ray

The color of the light is purple and gold and the creative qualities are peace and service. Obviously, the quality of peace has been perverted into all kinds of conflicts and war. Service has also been perverted into becoming either self-serving or the service of a cause that does not bring true growth. For example, one of the major causes of war is religion. The idea that there is only one true religion and that promoting it justifies the killing of other people is a perversion of both peace and service.

- The Elohim of the Sixth Ray is Peace and you invoke his energy to restore the vision of how to bring peace and how to give a form of service that raises all life (instead of serving a small power elite).

- The Archangel is Uriel and you invoke him in order to consume all forces of conflict and war as well as anti-service.

- The Chohan is Nada and you invoke her to bring change and vision into public service and activities related to children, youth and families. You also invoke Nada to help you attain personal peace and help bring peace to society.

You invoke the energies of the Sixth Ray into any institution related to public service and any institution related to bringing peace and avoiding war. The corresponding chakra is the Solar Plexus Chakra.

Seventh Ray

The color of the light is violet and the creative qualities are freedom and justice. Both the freedom and the justice aspect has been perverted on earth. There are obvious perversions of freedom that physically take away people's freedom, but there are many more subtle perversions that limit us through the mind. For example, the limited vision mentioned in the description of the Fifth Ray takes away freedom much more efficiently than iron chains. Justice has been perverted in many ways, including allowing a small power elite to be above the law.

- The Elohim of the Seventh Ray is Arcturus and you invoke his energy to bring a true vision of freedom and justice.

- The Archangel is Zadkiel and you invoke him to consume all forces of anti-freedom and anti-justice that seek to trap people in their minds.

- The Chohan is Saint Germain and you invoke him to bring not only freedom but also the knowledge of how to attain the mastery of mind over matter that is the foundation for true alchemy.

Saint Germain is the main master who oversees the Age of Aquarius and he has a plan for how to manifest a golden age in the coming 2,000-year cycle. This involves changes in all areas of society and you can invoke Saint Germain for help in any aspect of your Divine plan.

Seeing the need to do something drastic in order to bring about his golden age, Saint Germain received a dispensation to release knowledge of a special form of energy that is very powerful for transmuting fear-based energy and karma. Since the 1930s students of Saint Germain have been invoking this violet flame energy and the masters have released many decrees and invocations for this purpose. Saint Germain's Divine consort is Portia who serves as the Goddess of Justice. You can invoke her into the justice systems of the world and also particular cases and issues.

You invoke the energies of the Seventh Ray into any area of society related to freedom, justice, alchemy and diplomacy. The corresponding chakra is the Soul Chakra.

How the masters give us new teachings and tools

The tools presented in this book are not made up by human beings but are given to us directly by the ascended masters.

4 | A Closer Look at Ascended Masters

There is an old tradition in which certain people have been trained to serve as a kind of bridge or open door between the ascended masters and people in embodiment. These people have been called many things, such as prophets, oracles, mystics, seers, channelers or messengers.

When a person has been willing to follow the spiritual path and rise to a certain level, that person can be selected by the ascended masters to bring forth new teachings and tools. For millennia, the ascended masters have guided the growth of humankind and they have at various times used the opportunities available to them based on the current culture. The masters have a plan for bringing forth a progressively higher teaching and more effective tools.

The author of this book has been selected and trained to serve as a messenger for the ascended masters. The masters have given a large number of tools for invoking light, called decrees and invocations (currently more than 150 invocations). The masters have also given (and are continuing to give) new teachings. These teachings are brought forth as spoken "dictations" where an ascended master uses the messenger's consciousness to release a message that the messenger speaks aloud. The messenger is not in a trance but has raised his consciousness beyond the normal level and this allows the master to speak through him. Later in the book, you will find examples of the kind of messages that are given by the ascended masters.

The masters call this "progressive revelation" because as people respond to previous teachings and raise their consciousness, new teachings can be released. Progressive revelation has an Alpha and an Omega aspect. The Alpha aspect is that teachings are given that are more advanced than anything given before. This allows those who have raised their consciousness to a higher level to receive a more sophisticated teaching. The Omega aspect is that teachings are given that are easier to understand and can be grasped by more people. This allows the teachings to gain wider acceptance so that more and more people can see the value of ascended master teachings.

How to avoid being confused

When you first hear about ascended masters, it is easy to feel confused or overwhelmed by the complexity of seven rays and such a large number of masters. If you have been used to praying to one God, Jesus or Mother Mary it might seem like it is too much. It is important to avoid this feeling by focusing on one or a few masters.

By reading the descriptions above you may already have a sense of which master or which spiritual ray appeals most to you. You might look at the areas of society that come under a specific ray and thereby sense which ray appeals most to you. If so, focus on that master or masters until you become familiar with him or them and develop an inner sense of attunement with the master and the ray.

If you don't have a clear sense, it is recommended that you start with a simple program. You invoke the First Ray for spiritual protection for yourself and your field of interest. You invoke the Fourth Ray to cut you and all people in your area of interest free from fear-based energies and dark forces. You invoke the Seventh Ray to bring transmutation of all fear-based energies in your own energy field, in the collective field and in your area of interest.

Keep in mind that when it comes to fulfilling your Divine plan, it is very helpful to know about and invoke all seven rays. Any problem on earth is created from a perversion of the energies of several rays, often all of the rays. You may start by calling forth the energies of one ray into the condition that is dear to you. After some time, you may get an intuitive sense that it is necessary to invoke another ray for a while, and this can continue until you have invoked all seven rays. This will empower you to give the most comprehensive service and to clear away all perversions to the resolution of a problem or the emergence of new ideas in a field.

5 | WHY INVOKING SPIRITUAL LIGHT WORKS

It is important to avoid transferring the old religious culture to the ascended masters. The masters work with many different groups of people in many different ways. The old paradigm that there can be only one true religion does not apply to the ascended masters. It is not the intent to say that the only way to serve the ascended masters or to bring love-based energy into the world is by using the tools described in this book. The intent is to explain why the tools in this book have been given to us, how they work and why they are effective.

The material world has four levels or octaves. The energy from the spiritual realm first streams into the identity octave where it takes on a form that is much more ethereal or fluid than what you see in the physical octave. The energy then becomes more concrete in the mental octave and takes on direction and momentum in the emotional octave before it finally manifests as physical phenomena. In order to have the greatest possible impact, it is not enough to bring love-based energy into the three higher octaves. Only by expressing the energy in the physical octave will you have maximum impact. The ascended masters are by no means saying that meditation, Yoga, mindfulness or other spiritual tools are not important or constructive. They *are* saying that the most powerful way to invoke love-based energy is to use the human voice through the spoken word. Through meditation you can connect to the ascended masters, but thoughts and feelings are not physical. By using the power of the human voice, you bring the energy down to the physical level and can then direct it into specific conditions.

Sound is a very powerful force that was used by the masters to create the material world. For example, the Elohim who created the earth first formed a mental blueprint of the planet and then used the power of sound to cause energy to flow into this matrix. What makes sound so powerful is that it is an energy wave. As we have seen, creating a physical form requires forming a mental matrix and then causing formless energy to flow into the matrix. Energy exists in the form of waves, and that means you need to find a way to get energy waves to take on a certain form and momentum. This is done through sound that is based on rhythmic repetitions.

Planet earth was not created instantly but over a long period of time. The ascended masters have given us tools for using the same process that was used to create the earth. These tools take two basic forms, namely what the masters call decrees and invocations.

How decrees and invocations work

Decrees are shorter worded statements that usually rhyme. They often have a series of verses and after each verse is repeated a refrain. This gives the decrees a strong rhythm that makes it possible to give them quickly and with great power. Once you have experienced how liberating it can be to give such decrees, you will begin to believe what the masters say about their potential for transforming the planet. This is an example of one verse and the refrain from a decree to Archangel Michael:

1. Archangel Michael, light so blue,
my heart has room for only you.
My mind is one, no longer two,
your love for me is ever true.

**Archangel Michael, you are here,
your light consumes all doubt and fear.
Your Presence is forever near,
you are to me so very dear.**

A decree might have four, seven or nine verses. Decrees are specifically designed to empower us to invoke as much love-based energy as possible. In order to be effective, the energy must also be directed into specific conditions. You can do this to some degree with decrees, but the masters have also given a type of tool that is more effective for directing the energy.

This tool is called an invocation. It has a series of verses that often do not rhyme but describe a specific condition, asking a master to send love-based energy into it. In between these verses is a set of verses that are repeated. These can be decrees that are used as the backbone for an invocation. In this way, you use the rhythmic power of decrees while giving them a more specific direction. The following is a brief excerpt of an invocation that invokes the light of Archangel Michael and then directs it into protecting you from specific conditions in the physical octave:

1. Archangel Michael, I welcome you into my life, my mind and my energy field and I accept your Presence with me always.

> 1. Archangel Michael, light so blue,
> my heart has room for only you.
> My mind is one, no longer two,
> your love for me is ever true.
>
> **Archangel Michael, you are here,
> your light consumes all doubt and fear.
> Your Presence is forever near,
> you are to me so very dear.**

2. Archangel Michael, envelop my physical body in an impenetrable shield of your Blue-Flame Protection.

> Archangel Michael, I will be,
> all one with your reality.
> No fear can hold me as I see,
> this world no power has o'er me.
>
> **Archangel Michael, you are here,
> your light consumes all doubt and fear.
> Your Presence is forever near,
> you are to me so very dear.**

An invocation often has 36 verses, nine for each of the four octaves. The ascended masters know that at this specific transition period there are not enough people who are open to their teachings. In order for us to have the greatest possible impact, we need to use the most effective possible tools so we can invoke as much light as possible. This will ensure that our efforts have the greatest possible impact on the planet. You will later find teachings on how great of an impact decrees and invocations can have.

Even though you might be sitting alone in your home doing an invocation, you are not really alone. When you use one of the tools given by the ascended masters, you summon the Presence of the masters with you. It is not the power that you personally put into it that makes a difference. The authority you have because you are in embodiment is combined with the power of the ascended masters. The words that you say out loud become sound matrices that carry the higher energies of the ascended masters. The words are what is called "fohatic keys" because they form "chalices" (like the Holy Grail) that the light can flow into.

Why these tools are so effective

The ascended masters are not saying that decrees and invocations are the only way to invoke light, but they are very effective for the majority of the people on earth. The masters teach that it is possible for human beings to be at 144 different levels of consciousness. When a new lifestream first comes into embodiment on earth, it comes in at the 48th level of consciousness. The lifestream now has a choice to go one of two ways:

- It can make use of what is offered by the ascended masters, namely a systematic path for raising your consciousness by learning to use the creative energies of the seven spiritual rays (this path is introduced in the book *The Power of Self*). This path takes you step-by-step from the 48th to the 96th level of consciousness. The steps on this path are described in a series of books called *The Path to Self-Mastery*.

- A lifestream can also choose to turn away from the masters and walk the path on its own. It can then descend below the 48th level to the lower levels of extreme selfishness. Such a lifestream must then experience conflict and suffering until it has had enough and once again is willing to accept direction from the ascended masters.

Most non-spiritual people on earth are below the 48th level of consciousness. Most spiritually aware people are above. They are ready to follow the path of initiation under the ascended masters. Many are already following this path even though they are not consciously aware of the masters, but they can speed up their progress by becoming aware of the masters and taking advantage of what they have to offer.

The masters explain that when you rise close to the 144th level of consciousness, you do not have to use decrees and invocations. Your awareness makes you an open door for love-based energies most of the time. Every thought feeling or action brings love-based energy into the world.

Until you reach these levels, it is highly beneficial to your own growth and to the planet that you learn how to invoke light through the spoken word. There is still so much fear-based energy in the world that it is almost impossible to reach the 96th level of consciousness without invoking light through decrees and invocations. People who are below the 48th level are still so tied to the mass consciousness that it is almost impossible for them to rise above the 48th level without making use of the power of the spoken word.

Many spiritual people will have experienced making progress for a time and then sliding back. Many will have recognized an opposition to their progress, almost as if some magnetic force pulls you back into old patterns. This force is the fear-based energy that has accumulated in your personal energy field and which the energies in the collective energy field can pull on in order to hold you back.

The same happens on a planetary level where you also see nations progress and then be pulled back. There is much opposition to settling conflicts or bringing forth needed political changes. A more powerful tool is needed in order to break through the resistance to progress, and the ascended masters have a perfect understanding of the dynamic of earth. That is why they have designed their decrees and invocations precisely to address this problem. These tools are given to us because they have the potential to help us break through and make a decisive difference in the growth of this planet.

The ascended masters have truly given us the teachings and the tools that we need in order to fulfill our mission on this planet. All that is left is for us to be willing to make use of these tools.

Invoking light does not override free will

The ascended masters are practical realists. They have given us some extremely powerful tools in the form of decrees and invocations, but they are not saying that this will automatically change the world. Invoking love-based energy or spiritual light naturally will not override people's free will. What it *will* do is liberate people's will from self-destructive patterns.

As an example, most people see an obvious need to generate peace in the Middle East. As has already been mentioned, this is currently impossible because the various groups of people are so locked in the way they see themselves and each other that they simply do not have the option to choose a peaceful reaction.

The deeper explanation is that the people in the Middle East have for thousands of years generated huge amounts of fear-based energy. When a critical mass of energy has been generated, the energy begins to form a cloud or pool of energy. The individual energy waves will start interacting, much like water molecules can form a maelstrom or air molecules form a tornado. The energy begins to spin and this creates a centrifugal force that pulls on people's mental and emotional bodies. People are literally overpowered by the maelstrom of energy so they are unable to make truly free choices. They are pulled into making the same decisions that built the momentum of fear-based energy and that is why you see the same patterns of conflict repeated over and over.

In the Middle East (and on the entire planet), most people are below the 48th level of consciousness. All individuals below the 48th level have too little spiritual identity to avoid being overpowered by the maelstroms of energy in the collective consciousness. That is why they are pulled into reacting the same way people in their country or culture have been doing for generations.

People who are trapped in such a downward spiral cannot break free on their own. Someone else must step in and diminish the downward spiral until at least some of the people can break free. The only practical way to do this is to invoke love-based energy to transform the fear-based energy that gives the spiral its power. The most effective way of doing this is to use the decrees and invocations given by the ascended masters.

Once the spiral has been diminished somewhat, a few people will start to break free. This means they can begin to question why people continue to do what can only lead to more violence and conflict. After a few people begin to question this, and after more energy has been transformed, more people can follow. Eventually this can reach a critical mass that brings physical changes. People begin to see that there is an alternative to the old patterns and they begin to realize how much these patterns were limiting them and their society. Once people begin to see that it is possible to do better, most people will choose to do better. History has proven this although there are always exceptions.

Changing the planet without using force

The ascended masters are not asking us, their students, to go out and physically battle with other people. They are not asking us to seek to force people to choose a better way. They are asking us to use their tools to reduce the magnetic pull of fear-based energies so that people can see the potential for doing better. Once we have done this, we leave the choice up to the people because this is how we ourselves avoid making karma by seeking to force others.

Can this work? The ascended masters started releasing decrees back in the 1930s. You decide how much progress has been made in the world since then. You decide if this could have happened without a shift in the balance between love-based and fear-based energy. For more than 20 years before the Soviet Union collapsed, tens of thousands of ascended master students had been giving special decree services to bring an end to world communism. The services took place every Saturday and lasted four hours. The ascended masters are not saying this was the only reason for the collapse of the Soviet Union. They *are* saying that it could not have happened so quickly and so peacefully without these decrees. Invoking light is a way for the spiritual people to have a decisive impact on other people's decisions without deciding for them. We all know that even though there is a great need to bring peace to the world, it is not right to force other people. In fact, how could one ever bring peace by forcing others? What the ascended masters have empowered us to do is to use people's natural tendency to do what is best for themselves. By transforming the energy that blinds them, we set people free to have a higher vision of what is best for themselves. Once they have this vision, the majority *will* choose to act accordingly.

The important conclusion is that using decrees and invocations cannot be done from a state of mind in which you have a fear-based need to force other people. Because we are not forcing others, it can be difficult or impossible to see a direct, physical result of the decrees you give. How can you ever really know what people would have done if you had not given your decrees and invocations? How can you ever know how long it takes to invoke enough light to set people free?

It is important to keep in mind that "discouragement is the sharpest tool in the devil's toolkit." You need to know the workings of free will so you do not set your expectations too high. Invoking spiritual light *will* have a major positive impact on the world. Yet do not expect that you can see a direct result or that the world will recognize the importance of the spiritual work you are doing.

As you gain momentum on invoking light, you can feel how the light flows through the words you are saying. When you experience light flowing through, you will know this has a positive impact. You can then easily let go of unrealistic expectations and continue to give the service that carries its own reward. You will certainly feel a personal impact of invoking so much light.

Of course, as long as the ascended masters have messengers to speak through, they will give us updates on the results of our efforts. It can be very fulfilling to feel that you are working with masters in a higher realm and that you are part of an inter-dimensional effort to raise the earth to a higher level.

6 | HOW TO INVOKE SPIRITUAL LIGHT

The ascended masters know what it is like for us to be in embodiment on earth. They know we all have busy lives and deal with many physical challenges. They also know that we are living inside a cloud of very dense fear-based energy that affects us in ways that most people are not aware of. The masters have designed their tools specifically to help us have a positive impact on the world while at the same time invoking the light we need for our personal growth.

By using the tools given by the masters for this age, you can have a positive impact on the world by giving a minimum of 15 minutes of your time every day. Obviously, the more time you spend invoking light, the greater will be your impact.

It is important to be balanced so you do not overdo it. The ascended masters always recommend a balanced approach rather than the "crash and burn" syndrome. Some people become so enthusiastic about the power of invoking light that they spend as much time as possible, ignoring that this makes their lives unbalanced. Eventually, it becomes too much for them and they stop doing anything. The ascended masters would rather see you adopt a balanced approach that you can sustain over time. It is the steady invocation of light that has the greatest impact in the long run.

The masters have given us many different tools for various purposes. You can find a great variety of decrees, invocations, meditations and visualizations on the website *www.transcendencetoolbox.com*. You may take a look and find an invocation that relates to your specific area of interest. In order to avoid feeling overwhelmed by the possibilities, you can also start by using the four invocations in the back of this book. They are designed to give a general clearance of the four octaves in the material world. This is a good way to get started and then you can branch out as you get a clearer vision of where to focus your efforts.

How to give an invocation

In order to give an invocation, it is important to have the best possible physical conditions. You will be saying the words out loud and at a level like that of a phone conversation or louder. You probably want to be in a location where this does not disturb other people or elicit their curiosity. You also want to not be disturbed by sound from the outside.

You can do an invocation anywhere, such as your living room or car, as long as you can be undisturbed for the 15-20 minutes or more that it takes. You might want to put the kids to bed or turn off your phone.

You can give an invocation from this book or from your ebook reader. If you use the invocations found on *www.transcendencetoolbox.com* you can print them from a pdf file. You

6 | How to Invoke Spiritual Light

want to sit in a comfortable chair where you are sitting fairly upright. Your clothes should be loose enough that it doesn't bother you. You don't want to be hungry or in a rush to get somewhere.

The invocation has three main parts. The first one is a preamble where you invoke the presence of particular masters. At the end of this short section there is room for you to make specific calls that describe the conditions into which you want the light to flow.

After that is the main part of the invocation and it usually has four sections. You read out the first verse and then you read the rhyming verses that follow. Then you move on to the next and go through the entire section. In the end is a sealing where you ask the ascended masters to seal you and other people.

If it seems intimidating to get started, you can go to *www.morepublish.com* and purchase a recording of the invocation you want to give, including the ones in this book. Following along with the recording is a good way to learn the mechanics of giving an invocation. It also helps you build a momentum whereby the invocation begins to flow from your higher self. This will invoke the maximum amount of light. Although using a recording is a good way to get started, there is not only one way to give an invocation:

- You can read it very slowly so you have time to contemplate the words and give them with more feeling. This can give you time to tune in to your heart and give you a strong devotional experience.

- You can give an invocation with a louder almost staccato voice that can give you a sense of more power.

- You can give it faster and with more rhythm and momentum.

You can experiment to see which method you prefer. Of course, there is no need to lock yourself on one method as all have their uses. It is important not to become trapped in a particular routine but to have a little variation:

- On some days, you might feel more burdened by energy and then a loud, staccato voice can be good for breaking through the cloud of energy.

- On other days you may feel more at peace and then the slow, devotional way is good.

- Or you may prefer to do it faster, not so much to save time as to build a momentum where the words start flowing by themselves.

Regardless of the method used, you will probably develop an intuitive sense for when your words are "cutting through" the energies you are dealing with. This can especially happen when you give an invocation a little faster. You can get a sense that you are riding a wave of energy that is literally cutting through the fear-based energy around you.

When you learn to give invocations and decrees in this way, you can feel a great sense of freedom. This might not happen in 15 minutes, but if you set aside time to continue invoking light until you feel the relief, it can be a great experience. Once you have experienced that invoking light can take you beyond your normal state of consciousness by setting you free from the energies that normally burden you, you will know that serving the ascended masters carries its own reward. It is great to feel that you are making a positive difference for the planet while at the same time increasing your own personal growth and well-being.

More targeted sessions

As you gain more experience, you can learn to use decrees and invocations to perform a longer service. For example, you could set aside one evening a week to invoke light for a couple of hours or more. You can then choose the invocations and decrees that are best suited for your particular area of interest.

For example, if you wanted to give a session for world peace, you might start giving 15 minutes of decrees to Archangel Michael to invoke protection for yourself and others. You can then give one or more invocations for peace (see *www.transcendencetoolbox.com*). Then give 15 minutes of decrees to Elohim Astrea in order to cut people free from the forces of anti-peace. You then give one or more invocations and end up with 15-30 minutes of decrees that invoke the violet flame or the Seventh Ray.

You could also give the decrees to Archangel Michael and then two of the invocations in this book. Then give decrees to Astrea followed by the other two invocations. End with 15-30 minutes of decrees to the violet flame.

On *www.transcendencetoolbox.com* you will find that there is an ongoing vigil where people around the world give the same invocations and decrees for a period of time, such as a month. There are also other ongoing vigils for specific purposes.

It is always powerful to invoke light with other people because the ascended masters multiply the effect exponentially with the number of people that participate. The most powerful effect is when people are together in a physical location and if you participate in a local spiritual group, you can try using the decrees and invocations together. There are also regular conferences held by ascended master organizations.

A good alternative to being physically together is to give the same decrees and invocations as other people. This can be at the same time or at least during the same time period. Again, see *www.transcendencetoolbox.com* for specific vigils.

7 | UNDERSTANDING THE PLANETARY DYNAMIC

The purpose of this chapter is to give you a different perspective on this planet and why you might have chosen to embody here at this critical time. As we grow up, we often accept the subtle idea that this planet is the only planet in the universe with intelligent life and that life can only be the way it is on earth. The ascended masters tell us that earth is a very small planet in a very large universe. There are millions of planets with intelligent life and most of them have been raised by their inhabitants to a much higher level than earth.

For a spiritual person it is important to know that you have embodied on a very dense and difficult planet. This can help you avoid the reaction of not wanting to deal with or take part in society. Many spiritual people sense something is wrong with this planet and this gives rise to a desire to withdraw from normal life. We dream of living in a better world, a world we have an intuitive sense must exist somewhere. The ascended masters tell us there *is* a better world beyond the earth so our intuition is correct.

The masters tell us that many of us have either come from planets with a higher level of consciousness or we have an inner memory of life in the spiritual realm. They also tell us that we have volunteered to embody on earth at this time because this planet is going through a critical transition phase. Over a very long period of time, the ascended masters have carefully worked with people in embodiment in order to raise the earth to the point where there is a potential for manifesting a golden age. Many spiritual people have volunteered to take embodiment here in order to help bring forth this golden age. If this cosmic experiment is successful, the model will be used on other planets with a similar level of consciousness as earth.

Before we took embodiment, we had a higher level of awareness and we clearly saw how dense and difficult this planet is. We also saw the potential we have for making a decisive difference, and that is why we volunteered to embody here. Unfortunately, once we enter a dense physical body, we often forget this perspective. We can be so overwhelmed by the dense energies and people's behavior that we forget why we came here. The ascended masters give their teachings in order to help us reconnect to who we are and why we came to this planet.

The masters explain that while the earth was created in a pure state, it did at one point descend into a downward spiral. In order to break up the collective consciousness that created this spiral, the masters allowed the embodiment of beings from other planets. Some of these beings had a higher level of consciousness than common on earth and some had a lower consciousness. Some were in a very selfish state of consciousness, close to the lowest level allowed on earth.

Although it may sound strange, even those with a lower consciousness helped break up the limited perspective of the original inhabitants of earth. The problem on earth was that

7 | Understanding the Planetary Dynamic

the inhabitants were so alike that they validated each others limited beliefs. The self-centered beings challenged the beliefs that had caused the inhabitants to close their minds and create a downward spiral. The masters say these selfish beings often form a power elite that seek to control the general population. The selfish beings are not truly powerful because they are being controlled by certain dark forces in the three higher octaves. For a more detailed description of such dark forces, see *Cosmology of Evil*. We who are the spiritual people need to know about the more selfish beings, normally called fallen beings, for three reasons:

- We need to avoid being pulled into the conflicts created by these people. We need to avoid fighting them or submitting to them. The ascended masters have given many teachings aimed at helping us avoid such dualistic conflicts, including *The Art of Non-War*.

- We need to recognize that we are here to pull the earth to a level of consciousness where selfish beings can no longer embody here. We do this by accepting that we have the authority and the right to be spiritual and to express our spirituality.

- By knowing that there are people and forces that work against spiritual progress (personal and planetary), we can avoid becoming discouraged or feeling hopeless about our ability to change the world. We can know that by becoming open doors for the ascended masters, we can help remove all darkness from earth and this will set the foundation for the manifestation of a golden age. We fulfill this goal by raising our consciousness and by invoking spiritual light.

The basic dynamic on earth is relatively simple. The earth will either be pulled up by the most spiritual people or pulled down by the most selfish people. The eighty percent of the general population will follow those who seem most decisive.

As explained earlier, the author of this book has been trained to serve as a messenger for the ascended masters. The masters have brought forth hundreds of messages (called dictations) through him. The rest of this chapter will present a few excerpts of these dictations. The excerpts are selected in order to give you a different perspective on the earth and the potential you have for making a difference.

Earth is a planet with much anti-love

Below are some excerpts from a dictation given by the Ascended Master Mother Mary. She holds the Office of the Divine Mother for this planet.

Mother Mary: You have – for a long time – embodied in a world that is not only devoid of love but is filled with anti-love. It is impossible to be in this world without being wounded, without being hurt, by those who are so trapped in anti-love that they actually feel threatened by anyone who expresses love.

When they are exposed to those who express love, they feel they have to somehow silence them, beat them down, stop the flow of love through them so that they can overcome the sense of panic that literally makes them believe they will die if they receive true love.

…

You who are the spiritual people should realize that you have come here as a sacrifice. You came here because you

7 | Understanding the Planetary Dynamic

desired to descend into this world where so many beings had become trapped in anti-love. You wanted to bring the sunlight of love in order to give them an opportunity to experience that there is something beyond anti-love. When you look at this, you can realize that you volunteered to come into a situation that you knew would be very difficult. You knew that your love would be rejected, you knew that you would be hurt and bruised.

I am not saying this to justify the hurt, to justify the abuse. I am saying it because when you accept the reality of this planet, you can overcome the very dysfunctional and non-productive attitude of feeling that you should not have been treated this way, that something is wrong, perhaps even feeling: "God should not have allowed this to happen to me."

When you go into that frame of mind – of feeling that some injustice has been done to you on earth, possibly even that God has been unjust towards you – then you inevitably become a victim of the consciousness of anti-love that you came here to eradicate.

...

I realize you are in this world and you look at life and the universe from inside the mental box of this world. I tell you that you did not come here, you did not decide to descend here, with the limited perspective you have now. Even though you may have been bruised and hurt and have shut off the flow of God's love and feel abandoned by God, I can assure you that you came here out of love.

...

When you are in a human body, you have certain human imperfections, but so what? They are all unreal, they can all be transcended, they can all be left behind. There is not one of you who cannot transcend your imperfections. You can only transcend them by letting them go. You can only let them go when you know that there is going to be something to take their place, something that is more than the imperfection. You can only know that through love.

When you reconnect to the original love, you also reconnect to the source of that love, and therefore you know that you came from that source. You know that you are infinitely more than your present sense of identity.

Think about distant galaxies and the vastness of this physical universe, and see how it gives you a different perspective. You realize how small the earth is compared to the vastness of the physical universe. When you reconnect to your original love, you take that broader perspective to an even higher level. You magnify it a billion, billion times. God's love is infinitely greater than the vastness of the material universe and so you have an entirely different perspective.

It is through that perspective that you can see how ridiculously insignificant are these things that you have held on to on this planet and that other people hold on to. That is when you can let them go and that is when you can reconnect to your original purpose. When the angel of God appears to you within your heart – in the form of your Christ Self – to remind you that it is time to start some aspect of your own Divine plan then – instead of rejecting it, instead of explaining it away, instead of finding some clever reasoning why you cannot possibly do this now, perhaps in 10,000 lifetimes but not today – instead of this reaction you can simply come to that point of surrender and say: "Oh Lord, be it unto me according to thy will."

You realize that the Lord is not the remote being in the sky who is seeking to force his will upon you. The Lord truly is your own higher being. You are only being reminded of the higher choices you made when you had the broader perspective that has been lost as you entered the denseness of this world.

You have a right to call forth God's will

Excerpt from another dictation by Mother Mary:

My beloved hearts, contrast the beauty of nature with the ugliness created by man in some areas. Then realize that God's will is that this planet expresses only beauty, love, peace and harmony. It is not God's will that there should be conflict, pain and suffering on earth. When you realize this truth, you realize that you, as the son or daughter of God, have an absolute right, given to you by God, to take a stand for truth on earth, to take a stand for God's will, to take a stand for love, peace and harmony. You have a right to call forth the will of God to consume the anti-will of the egos of humankind and the anti-will of the forces of darkness that think they own this planet.

You have a right to say: "No more! I will separate myself from the anti-will and from all darkness. And I will *be* the will of God manifest on earth." You have a right to demand that God's will consumes the darkness, the pain and the suffering, restoring God's kingdom, God's peace, God's harmony and God's love to Mother Earth and all of her children.

My beloved hearts, if you love me, use my invocations to set earth free from the anti-will. Set your brothers and sisters free from the anti-will. Set your own souls free from the anti-will. Heaven is waiting for the authority to clean up this planet, yet that authority must come from *you*.

You are part of a hierarchy of spiritual beings

This is an excerpt from a dictation by the Presence of Infinite Light:

I come to help you understand that the one thing that provides a way out of the current situation on earth is spiritual fire. The spiritual fire can truly consume all of humankind's miscreations and misqualified energy before those energies become so dense that form itself begins to collapse under its own weight.

...

The key is to invoke the spiritual light from Above, and you have been given extremely powerful invocations for doing this very task. Yet there are many other spiritual rituals, from other spiritual traditions, that are suited for this task.

Beyond using the outer ritual, it is necessary and important that you understand that the light invoked is not simply a mechanical thing. Invoking light is not a *mechanical* process; it is very much a *creative* process. It will be ultimately effective only when you see yourself not as a human being, who is separated from the spiritual realm, but as an extension of the spiritual realm, as an extension of the hierarchy of spiritual beings that we are. You need to understand that this hierarchy reaches all the way back to God itself.

...

For you to be ultimately effective in invoking the light of God, you must shift your awareness until you begin to realize and accept that you are a part of the hierarchy of self-conscious beings, of co-creators with God, that reaches all the way back to your Creator.

Pessimists will not manifest the Golden Age

Excerpts from a dictation by Saint Germain who is the master overseeing the Aquarian age. He is the one holding the blueprint for a golden age on earth:

It is a new day. If you cannot sense my joy and my optimism, then I suggest you do some serious rethinking. It will not be pessimists or fatalists who will build the Golden Age of Saint Germain. It will be the optimists who are willing to question their mental boxes and question every idea that puts a limitation on the creativity of God, expressed through the individualizations of God. *That* is the final sentence.

The Golden Age will be built by those who are willing to acknowledge that with God all things are possible—when the creativity of God is expressed through the individualizations of God.

...

I look forward to speaking to you many times in the years to come. I have much to unveil about the Golden Age of Aquarius. I am anxious, I am eager, I am filled with joy at the prospect of unveiling my vision for those who have eyes to see.

Open your eyes, and you shall see Saint Germain's vision for the Golden Age of Aquarius. Oh what a vision it is, oh what a vision it is. Not fashioned exclusively by me, but by the entire spirit of the ascended masters who work with planet earth. It starts at the central sun, filters down through cosmic beings, through Archangels and Elohim, through ascended masters, holding various offices, through the Lord of the World, Gautama Buddha, through the Cosmic Christ, Maitreya, through the individualized Christ, Jesus, through that beloved being, Mother Mary. And then through the office that I hold, that of the Hierarch of the Age of Aquarius.

Positive ideas are released by ascended masters

Excerpts from a dictation by Saint Germain:

Every positive change that has happened on this planet started with an idea released from the realm of the ascended masters, which then descended through the four levels of the material universe—the identity, mental, emotional and physical realms.

We are constantly releasing such ideas, but they will not have an effect in the physical until one or more people grasp that ascended master idea with their outer awareness. They either start expressing it as an idea of what needs to change, or start expressing it as a practical innovation, as a practical invention, that suddenly brings forth a technology that revolutionizes some aspect of society.

What we are looking for is that more and more people will be able to tune in to the ideas we are releasing. As Jesus said 2,000 years ago: "Fear not little flock, for it is the Father's good pleasure to give you the kingdom." The Father's good pleasure is executed by the ascended masters who are working with humankind on earth.

We, the ascended masters, have solutions to every problem you find on planet earth. The catch is, my beloved, that those solutions cannot be given unless people are willing to change their consciousness. You cannot solve a problem with the same state of consciousness that created or precipitated the problem. This is simply not possible. That is why it is essential that the consciousness shifts so that people can reach beyond the old way of looking at a particular problem and be open to receiving the solution.

What you have seen in the past is that typically one person was able to raise his or her consciousness, tune in to the ascended masters and receive an idea—whether it be a political or spiritual idea, or a practical idea about a particular invention. You have also seen a few instances where two people independently of each other made the same discovery or came forth with the same invention.

What we are looking for is a situation where so many people are open and attuned to the ascended masters that many people at the same time – all across the planet – will tune in to a particular idea. This is especially important when it comes to ideas about political changes or spiritual changes where it is not enough that one person brings forth a technical invention, but where many people need to catch on to an idea before it will begin to have an impact on society.

...

In the Aquarian age, we need thousands, and tens of thousands and millions of people to be so attuned with the new ideas we are releasing that many of the people catch that idea as soon as it is released and immediately start speaking about it. All around the world there is a mushrooming in the awareness that something has changed or something needs to change. There is a new awareness and a new determination that these old problems are no longer acceptable to us and we want a change and we want it *now*. Not because somebody says so, but because we say so because we know in our hearts that this is true, that this is right, that this is necessary.

We are not looking at the Aquarian age as an age in which we have a few remarkable leaders, but where we have millions of remarkable people who dare to stand up and speak the truth that they know in their hearts—even if they cannot argue for it in rational, analytical terms, or by pointing to any outer authority, but simply by speaking out from their hearts.

8 | THE EFFECT OF INVOKING SPIRITUAL LIGHT

This chapter contains excerpts from ascended master dictations that explain the effect it has when we invoke spiritual light. The masters also comment on the effect of the invocations and decrees they have released.

Invocations produce very powerful sound waves

Excerpt from a dictation by Saint Germain:
   I can assure you that as you give an invocation, you are sending the vibration of sound into the mass consciousness and the four levels of the material universe. I can assure you that the effect of your invocations is very dramatic and, I might add, it is very beautiful as well. When you come into unison, when you speak with one voice, you create a very powerful unified and harmonious pattern.
   One of the greatest problems on earth is the multitude of sound waves that are crisscrossing the

ethers—that are chaotic, uncoordinated. It is precisely the uncoordinated sound that breaks down the organized, beautiful structures that are sustainable.

Part of the task of giving invocations and invoking the Light is to counteract the chaos. How can you counteract the chaos unless what you send out is more than chaos, is more harmonious, unified, and therefore sends out a unifying vibration? I tell you, my beloved, what science can also teach you is that you can have a substance, such as a gas, where all the molecules are oriented in all different directions in a chaotic pattern. Yet when certain types of energy are applied, there comes a point where – suddenly – a phase transition occurs and now the molecules line up and there is oneness.

This is what needs to happen for this nation of America to be one nation under God. There must be a certain unison in the consciousness of the people. As they say: "United we stand; divided we fall." America has fallen far below the immaculate concept that I hold for this nation. What will bring her back, except there is some unifying force, even beyond what people are aware of at the conscious level?

That force is not just the sound that is expressed. For it to have the full effect, the sound, the Word that you speak, must be infused with the Spirit. Thereby it becomes the Living Word, rather than a rote repetition that really is not infused with the Spirit and therefore doesn't have the power and the momentum to cut through the chaos of the mass consciousness.

That is why we have talked about the importance of the WORD, the Living Word. When you come together as a group, the effect of your invocations and your being together is in direct proportion to the degree of unity and oneness you can attain. How can you attain oneness? You can do so only when a critical mass of people in the group reach for the Living Word within themselves.

...

When you let go of the ego, you can come into a oneness where you have a oneness within you with the Living Word. Even though you sit here in a group – and you all say the same words in the invocation, you all say them with the same speed and in the same rhythm – the words you say are not just mechanical words. Each one of you is endowing your words with your heart flame, with your God Flame. Even though the words might sound the same, I can assure you that the vibrational pattern that is sent out is endowed with the unique qualities of each person's God Flame.

Invocations reinforce people doing physical work

Excerpt from a dictation by Mother Mary:

My beloved hearts, I come to give you the gratitude of Heaven for the magnificent work you have done with the *Healing Invocation for Disasters* and the other invocations you have given. I want you to take a look at this disaster [The tsunami in Indonesia in 2005] and see that even many of the medical experts are surprised that there has not been a widespread outbreak of contagious diseases. These experts did, in their professional opinions and assessment, expect such diseases to kill as many people as were killed directly by the tsunamis. I want you to understand that had it not been for your work with my invocations, these epidemics surely would have come to pass.

I am not thereby asking you to in any way feel a conceited sense that you alone and the invocations alone prevented these epidemics. Surely, many dedicated healthcare workers were on the scene and took the physical measures that were also a necessary ingredient in preventing the outbreak of disease. Yet I must tell you that when someone on earth does the spiritual work, then the physical efforts of other people will have a far greater effect.

This is the principle that I desire you to understand by seeing how just a few people giving an invocation can have a positive impact on a situation as severe as the aftermath of the tsunami disaster. Your calls have also healed and consoled many, opened up ways to get critical supplies to the right places and made it easier for the survivors to start rebuilding. Your calls also opened up for more generous financial aid.

This should give you a sense of co-measurement of what can be achieved when those who are the spiritual people of earth use my invocations to reinforce the efforts of those who are taking physical action to improve world conditions. This should give you the sense that truly there are no limitations for what can be achieved in terms of positive change on earth, except perhaps the limitations you allow to linger in your minds.

Do you not see that you have been brought up, almost from infancy, to limit the power of God and God's ability to change this world? Most especially, you have been brought up to limit God's power to work through *you*. It is truly the greatest travesty on earth that those who are the sons and daughters of God have been programmed to deny their heritage, and thereby programmed to deny God the ability to work through them.

My beloved, do you not see that Jesus came for the primary purpose of shattering the illusion that God cannot work through a human being and bring forth positive change on earth? He came to demonstrate that nothing is too hard for the Lord and that with God all things are possible. You are with God when you go deeply within yourself, when you go into the kingdom of God that is within you, and find the God Presence that is truly deep within every human being. My invocations are no substitute for finding the Presence of God within you and I would never want you to see them as such. My invocations are guiding rods, they are a ladder that helps you climb into the kingdom of God within you. The invocations help you climb above the mass consciousness that pulls you down into accepting your mortality, or even accepting yourself as a miserable sinner who must passively wait for an outer savior to come and save you.

How Mother Mary's invocations can prevent a war

Excerpt of a longer dictation by Gautama Buddha:

As it is customary to do status at the end of the year, let us take a quick glance back at the year 2006. What were the most significant events that happened in 2006? The most significant event of 2006 was an event that did *not* happen, namely that we did not have the outbreak in the physical of a major war. Surely, you have seen unrest. Surely, you have seen the seeds of war planted. They have not yet sprouted to full fruition, as they truly could have done, had it not been for one particular factor. That factor, my beloved, is Mother Mary's invocations and the peace invocations that so many people have taken up during this year.

In the interest of not causing you to be tempted to be engaged in any form of superiority, I will give you a realistic assessment. There truly are not enough people giving these invocations that it can have the maximum affect that we desire. Nevertheless, if you look at world history, you will see that the first world war broke out after the assassination of one person. The shot that was heard around the world did indeed become many shots heard in many parts of the world. Truly, it was not that one assassination that caused World War I, for there was much tension between the nations that had been building for several years, but that one event was the catalyst, the trigger that caused hostility to break out.

My beloved, in those days it was virtually inevitable that a war would have broken out. Had it not been for that one assassination, then surely some other event would have triggered the outbreak of war. Nevertheless, in today's world the situation is different because the planet has risen to a higher level and the consciousness of humankind has been raised.

There is no absolute guarantee that a major war will break out. We are indeed at a point where the more time that passes without a war breaking out, the more likely it is that this will not happen. I can tell you that for each day that passes without the outbreak of such a war, the probability of the war decreases.

Had the trigger event that started World War I been avoided and had no other trigger event come up, then even the tension that was there would not have been enough to cause a war to break out. Eventually, that tension would have decreased and a war could have been avoided. I ask you to consider that the very factor that has prevented a trigger event that could have started a third major war has indeed been the invocations of Mother Mary.

When the pressure behind the dam builds, there comes a critical point where the dam is still holding but another few pounds of pressure could cause the dam to break. If something prevents those few pounds of pressure from manifesting, then the dam will hold until the rain subsides and the waters start to sink.

While a few people cannot have a planetary effect and remove all tension, they can indeed have the planetary effect of preventing a trigger event that would otherwise have made the tension that exists in the emotional and mental realms spill over into the physical. This, my beloved, is truly the significance of prayers, meditations, spiritual rituals of every kind.

Obviously, all of the people who have performed spiritual rituals have contributed to this event. One could say that there are other groups who have had a significant influence on the prevention of a war. While this is true, it must also be said that had any one of these groups not done what they did, then the trigger event would have happened. Indeed, as they say in the West: "The cat would have been out of the bag."

I do not want you to overvalue your service, but I do not want you to undervalue it either. I do not want you to become frustrated or attached to your service. I *do* want you to be realistic in knowing that you make a difference. This is a time when the few can have a major impact on the life of the many. If a third major war will indeed be avoided, then Winston Churchill's famous remark after the battle of Britain could be restated, and it would be even more true in this age, namely that never have so few done so much for so many. The spiritual people in this age are indeed the only reason, the only factor, that prevents this planet from sliding into the black hole of war.

What invoking light can and cannot do

Excerpts from a dictation by Saint Germain:

The main problem on earth is that so many people are unaware, are in a spiritual coma. As Mother Mary has explained, it is indeed imperative that humankind is awakened to the reality of the connection between people's consciousness, between the mass consciousness, and natural disasters. There are certain disasters that can be consumed through invocations and prayer work and there are other disasters that cannot be consumed no matter how many prayers or invocations you might give. This latest hurricane [Hurricane Katrina in New Orleans] is a typical example of a disaster that could *not* have been averted by the giving of invocations. The only thing that could have averted or mitigated this disaster was an awakening—on a national scale and especially in the area affected by the hurricane. If people in the area and nationwide had truly been awakened, the hurricane could have been turned back through prayer work and invocations. It would have been virtually impossible to awaken these people to a danger that they did not believe could happen or could be as extensive as is the case. The reason being that these people were so trapped in the two extremes I described earlier.

The main focus for your invocation work should be the awakening of the people. You need to be aware that what you are doing with the invocations is to transform the energies and resolve the dualistic beliefs in the mass consciousness that prevent people from being awakened. You are in no way seeking to overrule people's free will. It is a fact that as long as people are burdened by energy and trapped in dualistic beliefs, they cannot make free choices. Removing people's burdens will give them the option to choose, but it will not guarantee that they will change their lifestyle. Your invocations can give people an opportunity to come up higher, but no amount of invocations can guarantee that people will be willing to change their outlook on life and their lifestyle.

You must be aware that although your invocations are essential for bringing in a Golden Age, you cannot guarantee the prevention of all disasters. If people are not willing to change through inner guidance, they will precipitate calamities as another opportunity to wake up. My point is that even though certain disasters can seem very negative, they can also be looked at as a part of the larger process that *will* gradually awaken humankind.

You might consider that what has been happening since Mother Mary released her invocations is that the entire planetary consciousness has been purified and raised. That is why things are far more fluid and why disasters can more easily be mitigated. You still have localized pockets in which people living in certain areas have not responded to the growth in the planetary consciousness. Your invocations cannot at the present moment penetrate all such pockets. For that to happen, we need many more people giving invocations and working on their Christhood.

9 | WHY INVOKING SPIRITUAL LIGHT IS SO IMPORTANT

This is a dictation given by Mother Mary through the author of this book. The dictation talks extensively about invoking spiritual light, its effects and how to avoid becoming discouraged by daily activities:

I AM the Ascended Master Mother Mary. I come on this Christmas morning to talk to you about a topic that most of you know quite well, but you are not always as fully conscious of it as I wish you were. That is why I want to give you some words that might stay with you and might help you to counteract one of the greatest oppositions to your spiritual growth.

I have, myself, been in physical embodiment on planet earth. I was in my last lifetime a housewife with several children. I lived at a time when you did not have the many time-saving technological wonders that women have in the kitchen today—or men for that matter, too, if they venture into the kitchen. I know well how it was to be in embodiment at my time. You may think that was a long time ago, but when you ascend, time ceases to exist.

I can as easily remember how it was for me to be in embodiment 2,000 years ago, as I can tune in to how it is for you to be in embodiment today. Back then, I was extremely busy doing everyday chores just to get the family life working. I know that many of you, both men and women, are extremely busy today. You do not have to do some of the very time-consuming daily chores that we had to do 2,000 years ago, but then you have other chores that occupy your time and attention. You do not have any more free time and free attention today than we had back then. I fully understand this.

The enthusiasm of discovering the path

I would like you to think back to the time when you first became aware that there is a spiritual path, a path that leads to a higher state of consciousness, a path that leads through stages, steps of initiations, a path that is directed by teachers that have no human, subjective interests but are only interested in helping you grow. I would like you to reconnect to the feelings you had at the time.

Most of you were not brought up with an awareness of this path. You were brought up either in a traditional religion, for most of you the Christian religion, or without having any strong religious family background. You were unaware that there is a systematic path of initiations, leading to a higher state of consciousness, and that there is a set of teachers who are not like any teachers or authority figures you have ever met on earth, for the ascended masters have no self-interest. We have only the larger self-interest of knowing that all life is One, and therefore, there is only One Self. The only way to raise ourselves, as you would say it, is to raise the All. Many of you felt a great sense of liberation, joy, and enthusiasm when you first realized that there is an alternative to the lifestyle presented by materialism or traditional religion. You felt liberated. You felt that a new world had opened up to you. You were excited and enthusiastic about exploring that world, including studying the teachings and, for many of you, also practicing the tools and techniques that we have given. We have now, for not quite a century but coming close, been giving specific exercises – decrees, rosaries, and invocations – designed to help you invoke spiritual light and direct it into specific conditions in your personal lives and in the world.

I know that many of you felt this sense of enthusiasm and joy when you first became aware of these tools. I know that many of you can remember, when you think back, the contrast you first felt between your former state of consciousness and then the state of mind that you experienced after having given a certain amount of decrees or invocations. You can remember the contrast between your normal state of consciousness and the sense of having raised yourself beyond it, of having purified your energy field, getting your chakras to spin in the right direction, to spin more quickly, to let through more light.

Many of you have known how it is to walk on a wave of light, to float along with a wave of light, after having given, perhaps several hours of decrees and invocations. Many of you felt that contrast, and you felt such a joy of being free of the normal weight that burdened you that you would give invocations or decrees for hours, just for the joy of feeling that liberation from the normal heavy burden of energy that you carried.

The challenge of the daily grind

My beloved, if you remember how this felt, then I wish to make you aware of one of the greatest enemies of your spiritual growth found on earth. It is simply what we might call "the daily grind."

The human mind, the human energy field, has an ability to adjust. This is in many ways a very necessary ability. Planet earth is right now a very dark planet, compared to many of the other planets in your galaxy and beyond. It is impossible to embody here without being disturbed by the conditions that you cannot avoid knowing about. Even if you do not see them directly in your own life, you see them in the media.

This, by the way, is one big difference between today and the time when I was in embodiment 2,000 years ago. Back then, we did not know so much about what happened in the world around us, especially not far away from us. Today, you have exploded on these colorful screens all of the news from all corners of the world. You cannot fail to know what is happening on this planet, whether it be war here, conflict there, the mistreatment of children, the starvation of people, and so forth, and so on.

How do you deal with all this disturbing information? Truly, if you maintained the full sensitivity that is normal and natural for a self-aware being, then you could not stand being in embodiment on planet earth. You would be so overwhelmed by the darkness, by man's inhumanity to man, that you could not – emotionally, mentally, spiritually – stand being in embodiment. How do you, then, survive? By using the human mind's ability to adapt.

This ability is centered around creating a sense of what is normal. The mind, in most cases completely subconsciously, creates a definition of what is the normal state in your environment. Once you accept that this is the norm, then this gives you a sense of equilibrium. It is this sense of equilibrium that allows you to survive in a given environment.

How the mind gradually accepts norms

Most of you are not aware of this process. Most human beings on earth are not aware of this process because it all happened gradually as you grew up. Many of you cannot remember how shocked you were as young children when you were exposed to some of the shocking ways that human beings treat each other. Perhaps, you experienced it personally. Perhaps, you were abused in some ways, either physically, emotionally or mentally. Perhaps, you just heard about it by the adults talking or through the media.

Can you remember, for example, how you experienced it when you first became aware that, on this planet earth, there is a state that is considered normal by many people and it is called war? As a spiritual being in embodiment, there is a part of you that knows that war is never normal in any environment.

Most of you have been brought up in societies where you were exposed to movies, stories, books and comic books about war. You were given toys that somehow depicted war: weapons, guns, swords and soldiers. You were given the impression that on earth war is part of the norm. Most of you came to accept this, and it then became part of your state of equilibrium. This was necessary because how can you live on a planet like earth without accepting that war is a possibility?

On the other hand, how can you live on a planet where war is considered part of the norm? There is something deep within you that says: "This cannot be right. There must be something wrong here." But you do not know what it is as a child. On the one hand, you have a norm that gives you a sense of equilibrium, but at a deeper level of your being, you know that this norm is not right. The question is: "Where is your personal balance between the norm that has been imposed upon you from without and what you know to be true in your heart?" If you had completely surrendered to the norm imposed from without, you would not be listening to these words or reading them. You would be a "normal human being" who would not dabble into such esoteric spiritual concepts as ascended masters.

Many people on earth have completely surrendered to the norms of their society. There are even societies where people consider it completely normal to see themselves as being in a constant, existential conflict with other groups of people. Surely, you can mention the Middle East, but are there not many other situations where two groups of people have been locked in conflict for so long that both sides consider this normal?

Even though the people on both sides are in a constant state of agitation, this still gives them a sense of equilibrium, a sense that they know how life works in their environment. Strange as it may seem, even a state of constant conflict can give people a sense of equilibrium. If the conflict was removed, they would feel disturbed, compared to the relative sense of equilibrium they have now.

The dynamics of a downward spiral

This brings us to the topic that we have talked about in various books and dictations. Once the majority of the people on a planet have gone into a downward spiral, how shall they ever escape it? The downward spiral is created because people have come to accept a norm that limits their creative abilities. These people are not being the open doors for the light from the spiritual realm. If there is not a sufficient flow of light from the spiritual realm, then the people living on a particular planet will go into a downward spiral. Sooner or later, the second law of thermodynamics, as we have called it, will destroy their civilization. This is what has happened on earth to many previous civilizations, even some that thought they would endure forever, for they were so sophisticated and so powerful.

How shall a planet escape such a downward spiral? It can happen in only one way: There must be a critical mass of individuals who are willing to challenge the norm in their society. This may happen in any number of ways, as I know that all of you have experienced this in your own personal way. Something awakened you. Something made you realize that what the people in your society and family considered normal was not normal from a higher perspective. It was not normal in the sense that this is the way things are meant to be, or this is the only way that things *can* be.

You were, somehow, awakened to the idea that, at least in one area of society or one area of life, change was not only possible, change was absolutely a necessity. Someone had to do something to bring change, and you felt that there was something you could do. Otherwise, you would not have been awakened from the norm that was imposed upon you as you grew up.

There are many valid ways to make a contribution to breaking the negative spiral and improving life on a planet. Many things are needed. There are millions of people in the world who have never heard about ascended masters, who have never heard about spiritual light or invoking spiritual light, but they are still making a positive contribution to challenging the downward spiral and creating an upward spiral on earth. These people do not all have to hear about ascended masters or invoking light. They need to be doing exactly what they are doing. Nevertheless, I would like to give you a vision of what might happen if more people heard about the potential to invoke spiritual light directly and consciously. My beloved, from where should they hear this? Can it come from any other source than *you,* the people who have already experienced invoking spiritual light? What prevents you from going out and shouting from the housetops? What prevents you from no longer hiding your light under a bushel, the light that you have invoked, the enthusiasm and the joy you felt from invoking that light?

How invoking light can become a norm

It is precisely the mechanism that I have mentioned before, which is one of the greatest threats to your spiritual growth. When you first hear about the teachings of the ascended masters, and when you first begin to invoke spiritual light, there is such a contrast between the state of mind you experience after invoking light and your normal state of consciousness. You have a norm that is common on earth, and suddenly you experience that by studying the teachings of the ascended masters and invoking our light, you can experience an entirely different reality that is so much brighter, freer, more joyful.

What happens as you begin to invoke light on a regular basis? Suddenly, your sense of what is normal for you begins to shift. After some time, there is no longer this contrast between your normal state of consciousness and the state you have after invoking light. This is because your general state of consciousness has been raised to a higher level and invoking light now becomes part of your norm. Because you no longer experience the contrast, you often begin to feel that perhaps invoking light is not so great, is not so important. You no longer feel the same enthusiasm and joy. Perhaps you slack off a little bit and do not give as many rosaries, invocations and decrees. Perhaps you begin to think about other conditions in your life that are pressing for your attention.

I am, in no way, blaming you for this. I have been in embodiment myself and I was for long periods completely overwhelmed by my daily responsibilities. It is easy to look back and read the Bible and how I interacted with Jesus during his mission. You think that I was always in that state of consciousness, always aware, always alert, but much of the time I was just like any other housewife or any other person in embodiment: completely absorbed in daily responsibilities. I am in no way blaming you. I am just making you aware that those of you who have discovered the power of invoking light are our best hope for bringing about real change on planet earth.

Earth is sustained by spiritual light

The simple fact is that what determines the future of this planet is the amount of light that is brought through from the spiritual realm to the four octaves of the material universe: the identity, mental, emotional, and physical octaves. We of the ascended masters up here in the spiritual realm have almost unlimited amounts of light that we are willing to release to earth. We certainly have more than sufficient light to completely consume any and all of the darkness found on earth. We could, theoretically, release this in one instant, but what would be the effect of this?

The effect would be that the light would be so shattering to people's sense of what is normal that they would not be able to withstand it. Most people would feel that their lives were completely shattered by the light, for they are so used to the darkness that it is part of their norm and it is what gives them a sense of equilibrium. The light would be so disturbing that they would not be able to handle it. This is why we are not allowed to release too much light.

As we have explained many times before, what guides the evolution of life on earth is free will, the free will of the people in embodiment. That is why the law says that, even though we have sufficient light to consume all darkness on earth, we can only release that light through the minds of people in embodiment.

Become the open door for light

You, the people in embodiment, must become the open doors whereby we can release our light into the four levels of the material universe. Only by you fulfilling this role can our light be released. Only when our light is released will the darkness be consumed and things will change. Phenomena like war will no longer be possible on earth. Do you not see that we have the light that will consume all war and potential for war on this planet? This could be done, theoretically, in the blink of an eye. In practical terms, it can be done in a matter of a few, short decades, if enough people became the open doors so that the light could be released in increments.

Do you understand the wisdom of letting the light be released through the minds of people in embodiment? This ensures that the light will not be released quicker than what people can adjust to. When you become an open door for a certain amount of our light to stream through your being, you can do this only by adjusting your norm so that you can withstand the light without having your sense of equilibrium disturbed. Because all human beings are connected, if you raise your norm, it will pull up on other people as well. Even though they might be disturbed by the light, they will not be overwhelmed by it so they feel that their world view and their equilibrium has been completely shattered.

When you adjust your norm, you make it easier for other people to adjust theirs. Those who are the forerunners for raising their consciousness are really the ones who determine how quickly the collective consciousness on earth can be raised. You are the ones who determine how quickly we can consume a phenomenon such as war, poverty, disease, old age or whatever you might have that needs to be consumed by the light.

Do you see that if you lose your sense of joy and enthusiasm about knowing the teachings, knowing the path, and invoking light, then you will not be as eager or as willing to witness to others what you experience? Then, the rings in the water will not spread as quickly. More people will not be awakened so that they also can invoke light. That is why I wish to make you aware of the tendency, that we all have, to be so overwhelmed by the daily grind that we adjust our norm so that we do not feel the enthusiasm and the joy that we used to feel. Therefore, we do not share it with others so easily.

A sense of co-measurement

I would like to give you a sense of co-measurement. Since the 1930's, students of the ascended masters have been deliberately invoking spiritual light through decrees. This was sponsored by Saint Germain and his release of the violet flame, but we have for many years also given decrees that invoke the other rays.

My beloved, there are several ways for you to be an open door for spiritual light. I am in no way trying to say that it is only ascended master students, who consciously use decrees, that are the open doors for spiritual light. It is not my intent to say this. There are many, many people on earth who have raised their consciousness to such a level that there is constantly a certain amount of spiritual light streaming through their four lower bodies.

Most people who are deeply religious or spiritual are the open doors for such light. Many people who are not outwardly religious or spiritual are also the open doors for light through their kindness, their caring and their compassion. The willingness to help others, the willingness to raise the all in a positive way without using force or violence, this makes you an open door for the light.

Regardless of your level of consciousness, you can be an open door for much more light by using the decrees and invocations given by the ascended masters. There are a few people on earth who have reached such a level of consciousness that they do not need to use our decrees and invocations. Take note that I said there are "a few" people at this level.

I am not saying that all spiritual people should use our decrees and invocations. What I am saying is that, for the vast majority of the spiritual and religious people, they could greatly increase the amount of light streaming through their beings by consciously using the decrees and invocations released by the ascended masters through various organizations.

Using decrees releases more light

In order to give you a sense of co-measurement, I would like to refer to what is happening at this time of year. The reason I am giving you this dictation on Christmas morning is that there are few events, in fact there are no other events during the year, when so much light is released as around Christmas time. This is because the many people around the world who celebrate Christmas put their attention on the same event, the same traditions and rituals. Although they do it in different ways, it still creates a togetherness among all who celebrate Christmas, whether from this or that religious tradition. Many countries around the world, even those who are not Catholic, broadcast the midnight mass from St. Peter's Basilica in Rome. There are over a billion Catholics who celebrate this together at the same time. When people put their minds together, driven by a positive urge, they do become the open doors for light in a greater measure than in their normal, daily lives.

You may look at these days around the Christmas celebration, and you may see that up to several billion people on earth focus their minds on this celebration and they are allowing a greater measure of light to shine through than normal. If you were to look at the earth with the vision we have as ascended masters, you could picture the earth as being dark, and then you could take one of these photographs taken from satellites during the night that shows you how much light there is around cities. You may even have seen photographs of how much the Christmas light has added to the normal streetlight in many areas of the world.

I can look at this from the ascended master perspective. I can see the normal level of the release of spiritual light on earth, and then I can see the increase around Christmas time. I can assure you that the increase is dramatic, but bear in mind that this is produced by billions of people participating in similar rituals at a similar time.

I wish to give you a sense of co-measurement. Let us say that we had 500 ascended master students, sitting around the world in their own homes, but they decided to do a four-hour vigil of giving the rosaries, decrees and invocations released through this messenger. They would do this in the same four-hour time slot. I can tell you that if 500 people were to use the tools we have given, they could release more light in four hours than all of the billions of people celebrating Christmas. Five hundred people, my beloved, could release more light than billions of Christians who are not using the tools given by the ascended masters, the tools that we have given specifically for this time.

You could take the tools we have given in previous organizations and dispensations, and they could also achieve very spectacular results, but it would take more people. The further you go back in time, the more people it would take to achieve this same result because our previous tools were not as effective for this time as the tools we are releasing now. The tools we have released through this messenger are Aquarian age tools. They will be effective for a very long time, although not forever. The tools we had given in previous dispensations were, to some degree, adapted to the transition between Pisces and Aquarius that those dispensations were meant to address. They were extremely effective tools for their time. They are still effective but not as effective as the tools that are specifically given for the first decades of the Aquarian age.

Consider, my beloved, that 500 people using the most effective tools available for invoking light could release more light than billions of people celebrating Christmas. I do not wish to limit the number to 500; it just so happens that this is the point where the balance would be achieved, the level where a four-hour vigil using our invocations and decrees would release more light than the Christmas celebration. Of course, if we had a thousand, two thousand, ten thousand, or even more people around the world who would invoke light, even if it were not at the same time, then the effect would be many, many times greater. [See *www.transcendencetoolbox.com* for information about this vigil.] I can assure you that when you look at the earth, anyone using our invocations and decrees will create a light that is noticeable. It is as noticeable as a very bright light would be for a satellite looking at the dark earth.

There is no wasted effort

You, of course, do not normally feel what I am saying here when you give your decrees and invocations. This is because you are inside the system of the earth; you are experiencing life from the inside. You are under the burden of the cloud of the mass consciousness and the negative energies. Even when you give decrees and invocations, you may still be feeling this, and in many cases, you do not have time in your daily lives to give the decrees and invocations long enough to consciously experience being above the energies.

I do understand that many of you have busy lives where you cannot give two, three or four hours of decrees and invocations in order to raise yourself above the negative energies. I am only telling you this because I want you to know that even if you give 15 minutes of decrees or invocations, it still has a tremendous effect, even if you do not consciously feel it.

There is no effort made by using these tools that is ever wasted. There is no effort made that does not have a significant positive impact on the future of both your personal life and growth and the planet. I am not trying to say that you should go around feeling spiritual pride and feeling that you are better than other people. On the other hand, I *am* saying that you should not allow the daily grind and the weight of the energies to make you feel that this doesn't matter, that it isn't making any difference, that who cares about what you are doing?

We of the ascended masters care very much about every human being who is an open door for the light. We care especially for those who are making conscious use of the tools we have released for the purpose of shifting the earth to a higher level. We see the significance of every minute you spend invoking light. It is not insignificant what you do. It is extremely significant.

I fully understand that you do not experience it that way. I did not experience what I did 2,000 years ago as being particularly significant. The difficulty of being in embodiment is that you are so overwhelmed by the energies that are so heavy on earth that you lose the ascended master perspective. We all experienced this when we were in embodiment. That is precisely why we of the ascended masters are giving dictations in order to give you that perspective, in order to help you awaken, at least for a time, to the greater perspective. If you did not have the greater perspective, you would just be living according to the norm in your society and then the downward spiral could never be broken.

I am not blaming you for feeling what you are feeling. I am only seeking to give you a sense of co-measurement and inspire you to know that it *does* matter what you do. Every time you take an invocation or decree and open your mouth, there are angels who are standing ready to take the light released and put it to the best possible use in raising the earth. When people come together for the Christmas celebration, millions of angels stand ready to take the light and put it to the best possible use. When you open your mouth to give a decree or an invocation, the angels are ready. It is never wasted. It will always have a positive impact.

The challenge of being in embodiment on a planet as heavy as earth is to know in your heart that what you do makes a difference and then continue to do it even though you do not directly experience the difference that it makes. I can assure you that when you leave embodiment, you will be shown the difference it made that you gave the invocations and decrees. Any positive difference you have made through whatever activity will be shown to you after you leave embodiment. I fully understand that this is not much comfort to you right now. I fully understand that many of you feel overwhelmed, especially at this dark time of the year where it is easy to feel alone and feel like: "Does it really matter? Does it make any difference? Is it really worth it?"

My beloved, it *does* matter! It *does* make a difference! You decide whether that makes it worth it. I have already made my decision, and I know it is worth it. I am eternally grateful for all those people who have used our decrees and invocations. I have now released over 150 rosaries and invocations through this messenger. More will be forthcoming, I can assure you. I do this because I know it makes a difference.

Even if only one person gave an invocation one time, it would make a difference, but my vision is far greater. My vision is that in the future thousands of people will come together, as you saw in St. Peter's in Rome yesterday for the midnight mass, and they will give decrees and invocations in unison. This will not happen in St. Peter's Basilica—*that* I do not envision. I do envision people coming together both physically and over the Internet and giving these tools, using them with full awareness of how powerful they are.

Where is the Spirit?

If you were to look at this midnight mass, what would strike you is that here you have one of the biggest church congregations in the world. You have this big, huge building. You have all these people coming together and all of these people watching on TV. When you look at this spectacle, my beloved, I have one simple question for you: "Where is the Spirit? Where is the opening for the Spirit?" Be honest and look at the people who come up to read, to preach, to sing. Do you see them being overpowered by the Spirit? Do you see them daring to be the open door and put some kind of feeling into their voices? It is not that you cannot be an open door for some light by being a good Catholic or a good Protestant or whatever. But if you dare to open yourself to the positive feelings of Spirit, you can be so much more of an open door.

Look at the Pope, my beloved, and be honest. He is the head of over a billion Catholics, but where is the Spirit? Do you not see a tired, old man? It is very understandable that he is tired, for he is carrying an enormous weight of energy, but where does the energy come from? It comes from the entire structure of the Catholic Church, which produces the negative energy that becomes focused on the Pope and almost knocks him to the ground.

There are very few people who have the spiritual attainment to be in a position like the Pope and not be completely overwhelmed by the energies focused upon him. Those people who have the spiritual attainment would never volunteer to be in that position, for they would know that they could not move the system, even with their spiritual attainment. They would walk away to positions where they could be of better use.

The Catholic Church produces negative energy

The system itself produces more negative energy than positive energy. I have said that a lot of positive energy is released at the Christmas celebration and it is true. Throughout the year, the Catholic Church as a system produces more negative than positive energy. This should be a cause for great concern for anyone who has an interest in the Catholic Church or the Christian religion at large, for the same is true there.

The Catholic Church is not contributing to the upward spiral on earth. It is not significantly contributing to the downward spiral in terms of energy, but it is contributing to the downward spiral by keeping so many people locked in a very limited worldview and a focus on these traditions and rituals that are not releasing light.

How can it be that over a billion Catholics are not able to feel that there is no light? It is precisely because the state of the lack of light has become their norm. Of course, thousands if not millions of people are feeling the lack of light, and that is why they are leaving the Catholic Church. Still, so many are locked there because they think that the way the church is now is the way it *should* be, or the only way it *could* be.

They think the lack of light in a religious organization or a religious service is normal. In fact, it gives them a sense of equilibrium. Look at some of the people who are sitting there in Saint Peter's on the front rows being on television. Look at how they feel important in their positions. This gives them a sense of equilibrium, and if the light came in to show them how hollow the outer position is, it would disturb their equilibrium. They do not want to be disturbed so they do not want the light.

Reconnect to your enthusiasm

My beloved, I am not saying this to lament about the state of the Church but to give you a way to reconnect to this enthusiasm you feel. What was the enthusiasm you felt when you first found the ascended masters' teachings? You may think it was that you got these wonderful teachings that answered so many of your questions, but the real source of the enthusiasm and joy was that you encountered the light, the spiritual light, in a greater measure than you had ever encountered it before.

Why do you, perhaps, not feel the same enthusiasm today? Because the level of light that you receive has now become a norm. How do you reconnect? How do you rekindle your enthusiasm? By raising the level of light that can stream through you so that you still feel the newness of the light. If you want to maintain your enthusiasm for the spiritual path, you need to stay ahead of your outer mind's tendency to turn everything into a norm. This is one of the simple secrets to experiencing the spiritual path as a joyful process, rather than the Via Dolorosa.

I admit, my beloved, that I could not always do this while I was in my last embodiment. Do not look at my last embodiment and allow your ego to say: "Well, if Mother Mary couldn't do it, how should I be able to do it?" You should, instead, look at my last embodiment and say: "But I am living in a different time where the energies are in fact lighter than 2,000 years ago. I have the teachings of the ascended masters. I have the tools that Mother Mary did not have 2,000 years ago. I should, if I am willing to apply my knowledge and tools, be able to do better."

Exceed your image of the masters

This is the difference between an ascended master and those lesser teachers who are either in physical embodiment or in the lower identity, the mental or the emotional realms. The teachers who are not ascended want to set themselves up in a position. Although they are talking to you about how you can raise your consciousness and do all these wonderful things, they are not really interested in you exceeding them or the idolatrous image of them you have built. I am an ascended being. I know that especially the Catholics around the world have built an idolatrous image of me in my last embodiment. I do not want you to be limited by that image. I want you to exceed it. I want you to realize that you can do better in your last embodiment than I did in mine.

How else shall times progress? Do you not understand that this is the whole idea behind progressive revelation and a progressive spiral of initiation? When Saint German qualified for his ascension several hundred years ago, he had reached a certain level of consciousness. There are those among ascended master students today who can reach a higher level of consciousness before they ascend. Why would that be a threat to Saint Germain? I can assure you: It is not.

There are people who have the potential to reach a higher level of consciousness in their last embodiment in this age than Jesus reached 2,000 years ago. Do you think Jesus is threatened by this? Do you think Jesus wants you to hold back and hide your light so that you do not overshadow him? Nay, my beloved. Jesus wants you to do the greater works that he promised 2,000 years ago that those who believed on him could do. That is how Jesus feels the ultimate fulfillment of his mission as a teacher and example on earth.

Shine your light

Do not hide your light under a bushel. Do not hide your enthusiasm under a bushel. Do not hide it from yourself, first of all, but do not hide it from others either. Dare to let your light so shine before men that they can see that it is not *your* light but must come from a source beyond this world for which you have become the open door. Dare to tell them that they, too, can become an open door for that light and that the best way to start this process is to use the decrees and invocations given by those ascended masters who have already become one with the light.

We have become the source of the light that you can receive, for no one in embodiment can produce the light. You can only receive light from above, and that light is not even produced by the ascended masters, but it is released by us in a form that you can receive on earth. There is no greater joy for us as ascended masters than to experience the light flowing through us and being received by someone on earth so that the circle, the figure-eight, is closed. The light that flows to you is put to good use to raise the All, and flows back to us whereby we can release more light to you in an accelerating spiral that has no limit from our side.

Try us, my beloved, and experience that we do not limit the flow of light. Grow towards the point where you can accept that you do not have to limit it either. Then comes that point where *you* do not limit the light, for you have become the open door, and you know this will make the earth more.

10 | TAKING RESPONSIBILITY FOR YOUR PLANET

The following chapters were all dictated by the Ascended Master Mother Mary. They were originally published in a book called *Healing Mother Earth*. That book has now been split into several books. The following chapters are included here because they give a good introduction to the concept that spiritual people can have an impact on changing the world. They also serve as a good introduction to the following books in this series.

Mother Mary: The books in this series are not for everyone. These books are released as gifts to those people who have been willing to contemplate the old saying: "If you are not part of the solution, you are part of the problem." These books are especially for people who have also been willing to contemplate the saying: "You cannot solve a problem with the same state of consciousness that created the problem." Once you ascend to the level of awareness where you begin to realize that all problems seen on earth are the products of a certain state of consciousness, you can begin to glimpse the fact that in order for humankind to find viable solutions to its many problems, there must be a willingness to reach for a higher level of consciousness than the level that precipitated the current problems.

Certainly, there are many people who would instantly object to what I am implying here. They would object to the mere hint that the problems you see on earth could be created by a state of consciousness. They have been brought up in a thought system which denies the role of consciousness. This might be a religious system that says the earth, in its current form, was created by God. It is beyond the powers of man to influence the conditions you see in nature or even on a planetary scale. It may also be people who have been brought up in a materialistic thought system that says consciousness is a product of matter, the matter in the brain. Consciousness does not have the power to influence the matter that is its cause.

These books are not for people who are stuck in the mental box created by traditional religions, nor are they for people who are stuck in the mental box created by materialism. These books are specifically for people who have begun to realize that there must be something more to understand about life than what has been defined in either of these mental boxes. They have begun to realize that in order for humankind to solve the serious problems you see on earth – natural disasters, environmental problems and problems in society – there must be a new approach.

These people have begun to realize that the approaches that have been taken so far to these problems have not brought forth a solution. They have either already realized – or could very quickly realize – that the only explanation for the fact that no solution has been found must be that human beings have not taken the right approach to these problems. If human beings are trying to solve a problem from the state of consciousness that precipitated the problem, is it not obvious why no solution has been forthcoming? If a solution is to be found, there must be people who are willing to reach beyond the mental box that precipitated the problem. It is precisely for people who have ascended to this level of awareness and self-awareness that these books are given.

Seeking knowledge beyond mental boxes

Who is the "I" that is speaking? I am a spiritual being, I am an ascended being. I reside in a realm of energy frequencies that vibrates far beyond the level of what you experience through your physical senses. I am speaking these books through a messenger who has been specifically trained to raise his consciousness and attune it to the higher frequencies in which I reside. I can use his mind and vocal cords as an open door for bringing forth this message.

If you are open to the existence of spiritual beings and if you are open to the possibility that we can bring forth messages in various ways, then these books are for you. If you are not open to this possibility, these books have nothing to offer you, as I will not in any way seek to justify or even explain my existence.

It is not my intention with these books to argue for or against certain viewpoints brought forth by the dominant thought systems of the Western world, namely mainstream Christianity and scientific materialism. My purpose for these books is not to present an argument but to present truth that can enlighten those who have already opened their minds to a higher understanding than what has been given in the traditional thought systems. If you are not among these people, simply go in peace, as I am in no way seeking to imply that there is anything wrong with you being in your current state of consciousness.

The simple reality is that the Word must stand on its own. The Living Word that I give in these books will either resonate with something within you or it will not. If it *does* resonate with something within your own being, you will recognize the vibration of truth in the Word I am giving you. If it does not resonate with something in your own being, then you will not recognize it as truth. You will therefore begin to argue against it with your outer mind. If you desire to engage in this exercise, I respectfully bow to your free will.

I will not in any way seek to cater to those who wish to argue, rather than seeking to *know*. Truth is beyond human argumentation—for one simple reason. Those who argue do so because their minds are trapped in a certain mental box. This mental box gives them a certain view, a certain perception, on the world. They believe that their view, that their perception, of the world is either the highest possible one or the only true one. They are seeking to impose and project their view upon other human beings. They feel threatened by people who will not agree with their view. They might engage in various uses of force in order to get other people to conform. This is what has created all of the religious or political struggles seen throughout history: One group of people feeling justified in seeking to impose their views upon others, even if it entails using violence or other kinds of force.

I am an ascended being, which means I am above and beyond this dualistic struggle for security. I have security in knowing who I AM, in having attained oneness with the reality that is beyond the mental boxes of human beings.

There are many people on earth, in fact millions of people on earth, who are also at the level – or close to the level – where they realize that there is a reality beyond the mental boxes defined by human beings, even those defined by the major thought systems of this world. These are the people who have begun to tune in – in their own hearts – to that higher reality. They may have different ways of looking at or defining this higher reality, but they all have one thing in common. They have glimpsed that this higher reality is made up of vibrations that are beyond anything in the material world. They have a frame of reference based on vibration itself, and this is what enables them to tune in to and acknowledge the vibration of truth in my words.

Consciousness can attain power over matter

I am an ascended being. The name that I have used in most cases, when speaking to human beings on earth, is the name "Mother Mary." This reflects the fact that my last embodiment on earth – my last embodiment out of many embodiments on earth – was as the mother of the being you know as Jesus. During that embodiment, it was my mission to hold the vision for Jesus reaching a certain level of consciousness and fulfilling the mission he came to fulfill.

Despite what you might have been brought up to believe, Jesus' mission had a very specific purpose. That purpose was to demonstrate the potential – that all human beings have – for reaching a higher state of consciousness. What exactly was the state of consciousness that Jesus came to demonstrate? It is a state of consciousness in which you have begun to realize one simple truth, namely that the human mind has the potential to attain power over matter.

Many people in the modern world have been brought up to look with either indifference or skepticism upon the so-called miracles performed by Jesus. These so-called miracles were not miracles at all. They were the application of a natural law, but this natural law will not work for people who are below a certain threshold of awareness.

When you are still stuck in a man-made mental box, you will not be able to make use of the natural law that Jesus applied in order to perform his so-called miracles. It is only when your level of consciousness reaches beyond a certain threshold that you become able to put this natural law into motion. Only then will your mind have power over matter.

This is truly what Jesus came to demonstrate, namely that the human mind has far greater powers than most people suspect. This ties in with my opening remarks about not trying to solve a problem with the same state of consciousness that precipitated the problem.

The problems you currently see on earth were all precipitated from a certain level of consciousness. As long as you look at those problems from within that mental box, the "solutions" you can see will all be defined by the mental box. You will be seeking to solve a problem with the same state of consciousness that created the problem. This cannot bring forth a viable solution. You will inevitably define the cause of the problem as certain other people. Then you will engage in a dualistic struggle to force them to change their ways, thinking – according to your limited vision – this will bring forth a solution to the problem.

Solutions require a shift in consciousness

When you look at the history of humankind, it becomes obvious that people who are trapped in this dualistic struggle have never brought forth true solutions to any problems. True solutions have been brought forth only by the people who are willing to reach beyond the mental box of their time and society and look for a new approach.

There was a time when most people on earth believed the earth was a flat disc. There were those who were willing to look through a telescope and study the heaven world. They used the mind's reasoning ability to see that something did not add up, that it simply could not be true that the earth was the center of the universe with the sun and the stars revolving around it. There were those who looked at other conditions known at the time and reasoned that it could not be true that you could sail to the edge of the earth and fall off. These people became the forerunners for a shift in the collective awareness that eventually caused virtually all people to accept that the earth is indeed round.

This is the only way to bring forth true solutions. You must rise to a higher level of consciousness than the level of consciousness that precipitated the problem. From that higher level of consciousness, you will understand the cause of a problem in a way that you could never do while you were looking at the problem from inside the mental box. From your higher perspective, the solution to the problem will become obvious.

This is the central message behind the mission of Jesus Christ. It was not a mission that was intended to be turned into another dogmatic church that would do what all the other dogmatic religions have done. It was intended to be a universal mission that could help all people rise beyond their present level of consciousness, and continue to do so until they had finally transcended any and all of the mental boxes created on earth. This was also what Jesus demonstrated when he gave up the ghost and rose above the level of energy that could be perceived by human beings still stuck in their mental boxes.

The entire symbol of Jesus ascending to heaven was meant to outpicture that Jesus rose to a level of self-awareness that is beyond what most human beings can perceive. This level of awareness is as real as anything you perceive on earth. In fact, it is more real than anything you perceive on earth.

The Office of the Divine Mother

In my last embodiment as Mary, the mother of Jesus, I fulfilled my mission of holding this vision for Jesus and his ascent to a higher state of consciousness. After that embodiment, I also ascended to the higher level of consciousness that Jesus rose to. I have since then been an ascended master, and I have now lovingly volunteered to take on a particular spiritual office for planet earth. The office I hold is the Office of the Divine Mother for planet earth.

This office has various aspects. One of these aspects is that I now hold the vision for all human beings that I held for Jesus in my last embodiment. I am holding the vision that all who are willing can ascend to a higher level of consciousness.

I am holding the vision that during this age – during these coming crucial decades – there will be a critical mass among humankind who will raise their consciousness beyond the mental boxes that have created the problems you see on earth. By these people being willing to be the forerunners, there will be a shift in the collective awareness. There will be an awakening that will be even more dramatic than what you saw in the Enlightenment, the Renaissance and the Scientific Revolution.

The potential for this present time is an awakening that is unprecedented in human history. This awakening can be an awakening to a greater awareness of the full human potential. The prerequisite for this awakening is that there must be a critical mass of people who are willing to go beyond their present mental box and consider the full potential of the human mind—or should we say the *spiritual* mind expressed through human bodies.

If you are concerned about environmental problems, if you are concerned about natural disasters, if you are concerned about the potential for the end of the world, if you are concerned about the economy or other social problems, then I can assure you that the only real solution is to raise your consciousness to a higher level so that you will gain a different perspective on the problems you see. By coming to understand the real cause of the problems, you will also gain a new vision of the potential solutions. These are the real solutions that will not only remove the problem but will help humankind rise to a higher level of the collective consciousness. Then the problem is no longer created and re-created over and over again.

The purpose for these books is to offer those who are open, those who are willing, a different perspective on the problems that relate to the physical planet upon which you live. If you are in any way concerned about Mother Earth and about the way human beings relate to Mother Earth, then these books will offer you a different perspective.

May you receive this gift in the same Spirit from which the books are given.

11 | OVERCOMING THE SENSE OF BEING POWERLESS

In this chapter we will set a foundation that we can build upon as we continue to explore the connection between mind and matter. Let us begin by considering your situation, as you are reading this book. The very fact that you are open to this book – a book that is claimed to be dictated by a spiritual being through the mind of a human being – demonstrates that you did not fall victim to one of the attempts at social engineering that you were exposed to as a child.

You may look upon many things that happen as you grow up in Western society and you may think they are relatively innocent. While they may appear innocent on the surface, I can assure you that there are many hidden things that have the specific purpose of limiting people's ability – and especially their willingness – to think beyond the mental boxes that dominate Western society.

Why are you open to this book? Because you have a natural curiosity about things that are beyond the mental box in which you were brought up. Why do you have this curiosity? Because you refused to submit to the programming that you have been exposed to since childhood. This programming takes many subtle forms, but just take the popular saying that most people have heard as children: "Curiosity killed the cat."

It may be that it was curiosity that killed the cat, but it was also curiosity that elevated humankind from the caveman stage to present-day civilization. When you look at the immense progress that has happened between the time of the caveman and today, you will see that the driving force behind all of this progress has been curiosity, the desire to know, the desire to understand, the willingness to ask questions beyond the current level of understanding held by an individual or a society.

Curiosity is the driving force behind progress. While there is a force that drives human progress, there is also an opposing force that seeks to hinder, hold back or restrict human progress and human curiosity.

The force that seeks to stop progress

I have talked about the two dominant thought systems of Western civilization, namely Christianity and materialism. Both of these thought systems are seeking to limit your curiosity in order to prevent you from asking questions that go beyond what can be explained by either system. There is an ongoing force that seeks to expand human understanding, but there is also a constricting force that seeks to limit human understanding to a particular thought system, to a particular mental box.

We will talk more about these forces throughout these books, but for now let me point out two aspects. One is the personal aspect. There is indeed a force in human psychology that has an insatiable desire for security. This force has been

11 | Overcoming the Sense of Being Powerless

known for a long time to modern psychologists and self-help experts, and it is commonly called the "ego." The ego is an element of the human psyche that seeks security above all. One of the ways that people seek to satisfy this quest for security – which is truly a quest for the immortality of the ego – is by adhering to a particular thought system.

In order for a thought system to appeal to the need for security, it must claim to have some ultimate authority. This is what you see in traditional religions, such as the monotheistic religions, which claim to be based on an infallible authority, namely the Bible being the Word of God. You see the same tendency in materialistic science, which also claims to have an almost infallible authority based on the so-called objective and undeniable findings of science.

When people decide to accept either a religious claim to authority or a scientific claim to authority, their egos can feel that these people are now secure in belonging to an ultimate thought system. This allows these people to put aside their curiosity, the questions that are not easily answered. An authoritative thought system offers you a sense of security by defining certain questions as being either beyond what can be known or beyond what human beings are allowed to know. You can live a comfortable life in the material world without having to be disturbed by questions that cannot easily be answered from the level of consciousness you currently have.

This allows many people to set aside or ignore their curiosity, but this sense of security is bought with a price. When you set aside curiosity, you will not only abort personal growth but you will also abort growth in society. I am sure you are aware of a period in history called the "Dark Ages." These dark ages were caused by the fact that the Catholic Church had managed to forcefully suppress all knowledge that went beyond its own doctrines and dogmas. The Catholic Church leaders had effectively created a mental box and then they had prevented the people of the time from seeking knowledge beyond that box. This is why even the material progress of society was held at a certain level for many centuries.

It was only when this mental box began to be shattered by the early scientists and astronomers that you saw a revolution in thought that led to the Enlightenment, the Renaissance and the industrial and scientific revolutions. Once the stranglehold of the medieval Catholic Church was broken, then human thought and human invention quickly caught up to the level it would have been at much earlier if the Catholic Church had not become a suppressive thought system.

Unfortunately, even science can be used to create a repressive thought system. There are those who have taken the findings of science and have used them to create a materialistic system that claims to have proven that there could never be anything beyond the material universe. This system has simply created another mental box that limits human curiosity. The system states that while you will not go to hell for eternity for questioning its doctrines, you will certainly be labeled as a person who is unintelligent and superstitious.

How cosmic cycles direct the flow of knowledge

The original mission of Jesus was to demonstrate the potential for developing the human mind to the state where the mind has actual power over physical matter. Why did Jesus appear on earth? He appeared because there is a group of ascended masters who have volunteered to take on the task of serving to raise the consciousness of humankind. We who are among the ascended masters understand very well the dynamics that is dominating this planet, even though that dynamic is currently unknown to most people.

We understand that the driving force of progress is curiosity. We understand that there is another force seeking to restrict progress by restricting people's willingness to ask questions. It was known to the ascended masters that, at the time when Jesus appeared, there was a need to bring forth new ideas and a new awareness. We are aware of certain cycles in the evolution of this planet, and we always seek to bring forth new ideas at the opportune moment when one cycle nears the end and another cycle begins.

The society in which Jesus appeared was a very restricted and restrictive society. Not only did you have the Roman empire, which had the physical force to restrict people, but you also had the Jewish religion, which had the force to restrict people's minds. Given that the two cooperated to a large extent, you saw a very heavy suppression, both physical and mental. The general population was held captive by a small group, a small elite.

This group, this elite, was not homogeneous but was divided within itself. Nevertheless, the different divisions were able to cooperate to some extent in order to maintain their positions of power and privilege. This suppression was based on a particular worldview.

There was the view that the world was very limited in size, and thus there was really no way to escape from the society in which you had been born. Then there was the view that the world was a very unpleasant place to be, but you had the potential to enter a more pleasurable realm after this life. Entry into this more desirable realm was restricted to people who fulfilled certain conditions, namely the conditions defined by the prevailing religion of society.

There was an elite of people who had set themselves up in between the population and God. The people could gain access to God's kingdom, but only by living up to the conditions defined by the elite on earth. Jesus came to challenge this view, and he did so in many ways. He did so by demonstrating that his mind had attained power over matter. If this had been seen as an example that all could follow, it could have revolutionized society. If more people had understood the essential message behind Jesus' mission – and had learned how to expand the powers of their minds – the Dark Ages could have been avoided and the Enlightenment could have taken place centuries earlier.

How did members of the power elite prevent the population from following Jesus' example? They did so by elevating Jesus to an ultimate and superior status as the *only* son of God. He was the *only* person who could perform such miracles. They created an elaborate doctrine and thought system that elevated Jesus to the *exception* instead of the *example*. This set the foundation for creating a mental box that made people accept that the powers of their minds were severely limited.

This mental box survived throughout the Middle Ages without being seriously questioned. It was only with the emergence of the early scientists that some people began to question the mental box upheld by the Catholic Church. Unfortunately – as science became more and more accepted in the Western world – the liberating power of science was severely restricted.

How science stopped investigating the mind

The emergence of science was clearly an expression of the expanding force that gives people their curiosity, their willingness to ask questions beyond the current mental box. The members of the power elite did not want people's curiosity to go too far. As the established power elite of the Catholic Church began to lose its power, you saw the emergence of an aspiring power elite who took control over science, or at least the way scientific findings were interpreted. This aspiring power elite created what is today the materialistic thought system, which claims that there is nothing beyond the material universe.

This system was based on a tendency to suppress knowledge about the powers of the mind. These early materialists attempted to set science up as being in opposition to all religion. They claimed that the obvious flaws of the medieval Catholic doctrines had proven that all religion is a matter of subjective beliefs that have no objective reality to them. They came up with the idea that only what was proven through scientific experiments – that could be repeated by anyone – could be considered an objective reality. They managed to make many people believe that the mind was inherently subjective, was inherently unreliable, and therefore should be eliminated from science as much as possible.

This caused a very peculiar condition. The very science that was born from curiosity had now become restricted from exercising curiosity when it came to the human mind. The materialistic paradigm managed to portray the human mind as the product of material processes in the brain. Science – or rather materialism – built upon the very paradigm set by the Catholic Church.

The Catholic Church denied the power of the human mind by elevating Jesus to an exception that no one could follow. The church denied the potential that the minds of so-called ordinary human beings could attain power over matter. Materialism took this denial to an even higher level by defining the mind as a product of matter.

Religion was open to the potential that a part of the mind could have been created beyond the material universe and could survive the death of the physical body. There was some opening for the idea that the mind could exist independently of the body. With materialism, it was now seen as an infallible doctrine that the mind is a product of the body and cannot exist before the birth or after the death of the body. It was also seen as an infallible doctrine that the mind does not have the power to go beyond the material universe. It follows from there that the mind does not have power over the matter from which it is created.

This is the contrast between the true mission of Jesus – which was an extension of the true mission of the ascended masters – and what the power elites on earth have been trying to do for millennia. We of the ascended masters are seeking to raise the consciousness of humankind, to raise the self-awareness of human beings, so they will realize who they are and accept the potential they have for taking command over the matter realm by using their minds.

Members of the power elites that want to rule this world are seeking to prevent people from rising to the level of self-awareness where they accept that their minds have power over matter. These power brokers are seeking to prevent people from coming to this realization so that the people will not use the powers of their minds to escape the control of the power elite.

The power of the collective mind

This might be a surprising worldview that you have never heard before. Or perhaps you have heard it in various versions. It is essential for you to begin to ponder this dynamic. It is essential for you to begin to ponder the true nature of the mind and the true powers of the mind. The current problems you see on the earth were created through the powers of the mind.

You may have been brought up to believe that natural disasters or environmental problems – such as pollution or global warming – have mechanical, physical causes. I am not denying that there is a mechanical, physical element, but the deeper cause is found in the collective consciousness of humankind.

Most people on earth have been brought up with a greatly distorted view of who or what human beings truly are. The reality is that you are not *human* beings, you are *spiritual* beings who were created for a specific purpose. You were not created to be passive victims of physical conditions on earth. You were created to serve as co-creators who would work along with the creators of the earth (the Elohim) in order to raise the planet to a higher level than the level at which it was created. Precisely because you were created to fulfill this role, you were given the powers to fulfill this role. Those powers are the powers of the mind.

Whether you realize it or not, whether you believe it or not, human beings are co-creators. They are constantly co-creating through the powers of their minds. Human beings are co-creating today and they have been co-creating for as long as there have been self-aware beings on earth.

The many imbalances and problems you see in Mother Nature today were co-created by human beings through the power of the collective mind. The fact that there are so many imbalances demonstrates a simple dynamic. The imbalances outpictured in nature illustrate the imbalances in the collective consciousness. Human beings have co-created these imbalances. They are being upheld – and even magnified – through the continued imbalances found in the collective consciousness. If these imbalances are to be removed from nature, then they must first be removed from the collective consciousness. This can happen only when a critical mass of people remove those imbalances from their individual minds.

Jesus came to demonstrate that one individual can change the world by being willing to raise his or her consciousness. As Jesus said: "If I be lifted up from the earth, I will draw all men unto me." All human beings are connected through the collective mind. Most people are severely restricted by that collective mind, which hangs over them like a heavy weight that limits their curiosity and imagination.

Awakening to your spiritual purpose and mission

Throughout the ages, a large number of individuals have demonstrated that it is possible for anyone to rise above the downward pull of the collective mind. When an individual does so, that individual will create an upward lift that will raise the collective mind.

There is a limit to the effect that can be created by one individual. Jesus was not meant to raise the world all by himself into some edenic state. Jesus was meant to serve as an example so that a critical mass of people could follow his demonstration. When these people collectively raised their consciousness, they would form such an upward momentum that they would be able to raise the consciousness of the whole.

This was the original plan for the mission of Jesus. That plan has not yet come to fruition, but there are enough people in embodiment today who have the potential to very quickly awaken to their true mission. Once they awaken to the potential for raising themselves to a higher level of consciousness, they can form the critical mass that will cause Jesus' mission to be fulfilled within a surprisingly short period of time.

Part of the purpose for these books is to reach out and awaken these people to what is the real cause behind their concern for Mother Earth. Your concern is a sign that, deep within your being, you have an inner memory that you have embodied at this specific time for a very particular purpose.

Part of that purpose is to raise your awareness to a higher level. You can become one of the forerunners for raising the collective consciousness to a level that will suddenly expose the essential dynamic I have talked about. This will enable the population on earth to come to see through the manipulation of the power elite. They can throw off the yoke of serving as the literal or virtual slaves for this elite throughout the centuries, even the millennia.

Why you are not powerless

If the earth is to be free from her current burdens, humankind must free itself from the burdens in the collective and individual consciousness. I am aware that many of the people who are concerned about earth and environmental problems have a tendency to feel powerless. What can one individual do when faced with problems of such enormity as global warming, pollution by international corporations or even the potential for nuclear war?

The central message of this book is that there is *something* an individual can do. *You are not powerless!* You have the power to raise your own consciousness, and thereby you will gain a new vision of the real cause of environmental problems. This will enable you to see solutions that you cannot see at your present level of consciousness.

The sense that you are now powerless is a complete illusion. If you will heed my words and use them to raise your awareness, the sense of being powerless will disappear. Instead, you will feel a new sense of empowerment. You will realize the truth behind a statement made by Jesus so many years ago: "With men this is impossible; but not with God, for with God all things are possible."

The truth behind this statement is that with the level of consciousness that most people have, many things *are* impossible. When you raise your level of consciousness beyond a certain threshold, then you will be able to activate the natural laws that Jesus activated when he performed his so-called miracles. When a critical mass of individuals raise their consciousness to this level, you will see a change in the physical planet. From a lower level of consciousness this will seem like a miracle. It is not a miracle but the result of humankind realizing that the true role of spiritual beings in embodiment is to serve as co-creators and bring the earth to a higher level of balance and abundance. Allow me to take you further into exploring the potential of the mind.

12 | YOU ARE CONSCIOUSNESS LOOKING AT ITSELF

I am sure you have heard the saying that history repeats itself. The background for this saying is that the ascended masters use various cycles to present humankind with essentially the same lesson in different disguises. Every time we present this lesson, some among humankind learn the lesson they are meant to learn. The majority of the people usually do not learn the lesson, and that is why the lesson is repeated at a future time in a different context.

With this in mind, take a look at medieval society. The ruling paradigm was the doctrines of the Catholic Church. If you looked at society from an official perspective, there was no alternative allowed. You could be severely persecuted, even tortured and burned at the stake, for questioning Catholic doctrine. You also know today that there was an underground movement of people who did dare to question Catholic doctrine. They existed in certain secret societies and they existed in the form of the early scientists who had begun to investigate the heavens.

Now look at the society you live in today. There is again, at least in many areas of society, an official paradigm, namely scientific materialism. This paradigm says that there is nothing beyond the material world. All beliefs in some kind of spiritual reality are simply superstitions that are created by the processes in the physical brain. Today you also see a kind of underground movement of many people who are daring to question this official paradigm. Fortunately, the punishment for questioning the official paradigm is not as severe as it was during the Middle Ages. It still requires some courage – especially for people who hold any kind of position in society – to question the official paradigm.

Even though many scientists are not willing to officially question materialism, there are scientists who have for decades been conducting research that clearly points beyond the materialistic paradigm. Let us take a look at some of the findings they have come up with.

Questioning the paradigm of materialism

If you go back to the 1800s, you will see that science had a clearly dualistic view of the world. The world was made of two separate elements, namely matter and energy. They could interact in various ways, but one could not be converted into the other. This is very similar to the monotheistic view of two separate compartments, namely heaven and earth.

In 1905, Albert Einstein created the first serious challenge to this dualistic worldview. His theory of relativity essentially says that matter does not exist because everything is made from energy. What most people have not understood is that, beginning in 1905, the official materialistic paradigm has essentially been shattered.

This is very similar to what you saw in the Middle Ages. When Galileo, Copernicus and Kepler started publicizing their findings that the earth could not be the center of the universe, the official Catholic paradigm was effectively shattered. Because so many people would not abandon the Catholic faith, the Church still survived and maintained a grip on society for a long time after these initial discoveries. Even today, the Church has a strong hold on the minds of millions of people around the world.

When Albert Einstein published his simple formula $E = mc^2$, materialism began to crumble. Einstein proved that matter is simply a construct of the human mind and the human senses. The dualistic paradigm of a division between matter and energy is clearly born from the physical senses, which are designed to detect only the energy vibrations that make up matter. To the senses, matter seems real, but there is a reason for this.

As a simple example, you might have seen movies of an airplane propeller, which seen from a certain distance seems to spin so quickly that it forms a solid disc. If you take the movie and slow it down, you become able to see the movements of the individual propeller blades. Then your eyes can see that there is space between the blades. It is a rotating propeller and not a solid disc.

This is the same way your physical senses work. Your senses are designed to detect energy vibrations that vibrate within a certain spectrum of frequencies. Your senses are not designed to detect the individual movements, the individual energy waves. Your senses are designed to provide you with the bigger picture that shows you the forms made up by these individual vibrations.

When you look at your physical body, you cannot see that your body is made up of smaller units, called cells. Neither can you see that the cells are made up of smaller units, called molecules. You cannot see that the molecules are made up of atoms or that the atoms are made up of subatomic particles.

Your senses show you a picture of the material world that is focused on the kind of vibrations that make up physical matter. Your senses are not able to see beyond that level of reality. Science has undeniably proven that there is a level beyond what your senses can detect and that this level is completely real. Science has proven the existence of cells, molecules, atoms and subatomic particles.

The world is a continuum of vibrations

When you take Einstein's finding that everything is made from energy, you will – if you apply simple logic – see that this has shattered the materialistic paradigm. The reason is simple. If everything is energy and if everything is vibration, then is there really any limit to what kind of vibrations can exist?

As an example, take your physical eyes. They can detect light rays that vibrate within a certain spectrum of frequencies, between red and violet. They cannot detect light rays that vibrate at higher frequencies, such as ultraviolet or many other frequencies detected by science. There is only a narrow spectrum of vibrations that can be detected by the senses, but science has discovered that there is a continuum of vibrations beyond this spectrum.

Science has also discovered many areas where there is a continuum that goes on indefinitely. For example, take a simple idea such as numbers. There is no limit to how far you can continue to count. Literally, the numerical scale is infinite, as far as science knows today. With this in mind, is it not also logical that there is a virtually unlimited continuum of possible vibrations? How can science then say that there is nothing beyond the material universe?

When scientists define the material universe, they define it in a very narrow way. They define it based on what they can detect with the instruments they have developed up until this point. This is really not that different from the medieval Catholic theologians. They had defined the limits to human knowledge based on their interpretation of Scripture and their definition of doctrine. What materialists have done is to artificially create a barrier, a boundary, and then they have said that human curiosity is not allowed to go beyond it. This is exactly what medieval theologians had done.

It should be no surprise that many scientists, philosophers and even many spiritually minded people have dared to think beyond the mental box created by materialism. Let me stay with science. Based on Einstein's discoveries that everything is energy, a new branch of science was developed. It is normally called quantum mechanics or quantum physics. This branch of science studies the very small, namely the atom itself.

Originally the word "atom" came from the Greek philosophers, and it signified the smallest possible particle that could not be divided into smaller units. Modern scientists have discovered that what they call the atom can be divided into units, namely subatomic particles. They have also discovered that these particles have some very strange properties. One of them is what is called the wave-particle duality, namely that a particle will sometimes act like a wave and sometimes act like a particle.

It would be more practical to no longer talk about subatomic "particles" but something else, such as subatomic "entities." It turns out that if scientists conduct an experiment that is designed to detect particles, then the subatomic entity will behave like a particle. If they conduct an experiment that is designed to detect waves, then the same subatomic entity will behave like a wave. Scientists are still baffled by this today, but it is because they have not been willing to think outside the mental box that goes all the way back to sensory perception. The senses can only detect something that has substance, that has mass. Scientists are still thinking based on this form of perception. What they need to realize is that the wave-particle duality proves the need to go beyond sensory-based thinking.

It is not that a subatomic entity can change shape and be either a particle or a wave. It is that a subatomic entity is an entirely different construct that is neither a particle nor a wave. This subatomic entity needs to be conceived of in an entirely new way that goes beyond particle and wave.

Questioning scientific objectivity

Before I go deeper into that, we need to take another look at some of the startling findings of quantum physics. One of the cornerstones of materialism is that science is entirely objective whereas all spiritual or religious beliefs are entirely subjective. This claim is based on conducting scientific experiments that will yield the same results regardless of the beliefs of the person performing the experiment. It is believed that the consciousness of the scientist has no influence on the outcome of the experiment.

What quantum physics has proven beyond any doubt is that this assumption is not true at the level of subatomic entities. When a scientist studies a subatomic entity, it is inevitable that the consciousness of the scientist will influence the outcome of the experiment. The outcome of the experiment is a product of three factors: the subatomic entity, the instrument used to study it, such as a particle accelerator, and the consciousness of the scientist.

Most scientists have not been willing to look at the philosophical consequences of this discovery. One of them is the fact that scientists can no longer afford to ignore consciousness. At the macroscopic level of visible things, you can conduct an experiment that is not in a visible way affected by the consciousness of the scientist. Everything that you see is made up of subatomic entities. The deeper laws that govern the behavior of subatomic entities will also have a fundamental influence at the level of macroscopic things. Since it has now been proven that the consciousness of the scientist can interact with subatomic entities, then it is no longer feasible to say that objective science can be conducted while ignoring consciousness.

The artificial construct that science decided to ignore the human mind cannot be upheld when you accept the logical consequences of quantum physics. This proves that it is absolutely necessary that science begins to study consciousness and the potential of the mind.

There must be something beyond matter

There are other philosophical consequences of the discoveries of quantum physics. One of these is that subatomic entities have no physical substance or existence. It has been proven that such entities can appear seemingly out of nowhere and disappear back into nowhere. From a logical viewpoint, this is not a feasible conclusion. Something cannot appear out of nowhere. It has been observed that a subatomic particle can suddenly appear where there was "nothing" before, and the only logical consequence is that there must be a realm beyond what is currently detected. In this realm, the subatomic entity can exist as a potentiality, but then something causes it to cross a threshold or boundary and appear as a physical particle. There are already many scientists who have begun to speculate about this realm. Some have called it a ground state, a quantum field or other names. What science has discovered is parallel to what mystical and spiritual people have been saying for thousands of years, namely that there is a realm beyond the material world. If you take Einstein's findings, it becomes very easy to see that this realm is made up of vibrations that are of such high frequencies that they cannot be detected by physical instruments.

There is a limit to what any instrument made out of matter can detect. A telescope can only see so far into space. Science has realized that the universe is so vast and so old that there are stars and galaxies that cannot be seen from earth because the light has not had time to reach earth. Scientists are aware of something called an observation horizon.

There is a realm of vibrations that has not yet been detected by science—and that will never be detected through instruments made out of matter. This does not mean that this realm needs to remain undetected. Human beings have another instrument that is designed to detect vibrations that are beyond what can be detected by the senses or even the physical instruments that essentially extend the range of the senses.

That instrument is the human mind. The human mind has the potential to liberate itself from the body and the physical senses. This does not mean that the mind loses awareness. The mind can travel into the realms that are beyond the material universe.

Throughout the ages, many people have developed this ability to a larger or smaller degree. All who are interested in this book have already developed this ability to the degree that they know – through an inner knowing that is beyond outer proof or intellectual reasoning – that there is a reality beyond the material realm.

The person who is speaking these words has developed the ability to tune in to a higher realm and receive energy impulses that are translated into words through his mind, brain, nervous system and vocal cords. Many other people have developed similar or different abilities to detect what is beyond the material world. If scientists would be willing to study this phenomenon – as some have already started to do – then there could be an entirely new field of scientific study that would bring about a fundamental paradigm shift.

Limitations of the Big Bang Theory

Let me briefly describe certain other findings of science. Quantum mechanics studies the very small, but the science of cosmology studies the very large, namely the universe as a whole and galaxies. Cosmology has proven that the universe is not fixed in size. Medieval theologians believed the entire universe was a very small dome that extended over the flat disc of the earth. Science has proven that the universe is far larger, in fact almost unlimited in size. Science has also proven that this universe is not only expanding, but it is expanding at an accelerated rate. Put this together with another current theory of science, namely that of the Big Bang.

The theory says that at some point in the distant past, about 15 billion years ago, the entire material universe was compressed into what is called a singularity. Then, supposedly, a giant explosion occurred that hurled all matter out from a central point. This matter gradually began to form various particles that organized themselves into atoms and molecules. Gradually – through a completely mindless evolutionary process – this formed the incredibly vast and complex universe you see today.

Scientists believe that this happened according to certain laws of nature, one of which is the first law of thermodynamics, which says that energy is always conserved. The total amount of energy that is available to the current universe was released in the Big Bang. No energy has been added to the universe since the Big Bang.

If it is really true that no energy has been added to the universe since the Big Bang 15 billion years ago, how can you explain that the universe is expanding at an accelerated rate? What drives this acceleration?

According to science, everything must be driven by energy. If the total amount of energy available was released in the Big Bang, does it not stand to reason that the universe should be gradually running out of energy that is available for expansion? If you take a bullet being fired by a gun, then all of the energy available to drive that bullet is released in the initial explosion. As the bullet travels away from the gun, it will gradually lose energy and eventually fall to the ground. If all of the energy available for the expansion of the universe had been released in the Big Bang, then it should not be possible that the universe could be expanding at an accelerated rate. The acceleration should have slowed down and the universe should have started contracting.

There is a way to explain this, and it is to take a look at what science has already discovered about the Big Bang. Scientists are aware that in the first milliseconds after the Big Bang, the laws of physics, the laws of nature that you see today, did not exist. They had "broken down." This means many things that scientists have not yet fully understood. What it means is that the singularity that preceded the Big Bang could not have been part of the material universe that you see today. There literally was no material universe before the Big Bang. There was no time, there was no space, there was no matter, there was no energy. There truly was nothing before the Big Bang that has any resemblance to what you see in the universe today. What, then, *did* exist before the Big Bang?

What existed before the Big Bang?

This is a question that scientists cannot currently explain. There is a logical explanation—but only if you are willing to go beyond materialism. The logical explanation is that before the Big Bang, there was no physical, material universe, but this does not mean that there was nothing. There was "no thing" but there was not "nothing." What existed before the Big Bang was a realm of frequencies that is beyond any of the frequencies used to construct the material universe.

This level of frequencies is what I would like to call the spiritual realm. In this realm you find conscious self-aware beings who have existed for a much longer time span than the material universe. This is not inconsistent with the consequences of quantum physics and cosmology. What quantum physics has proven is a clear connection between the human consciousness, the human mind, and the very basic building blocks of the material universe.

Today, you live in what is called an information society, but there are scientists who have begun to speculate that you actually live in an information universe. I have talked about a subatomic entity that can take on the form of a particle or wave.

What determines the form this entity will take on? What tells the entity to take on the form of a wave instead of a particle? When you begin to ponder these questions, you see that what Einstein did was to take one step towards a deeper understanding of reality, but he did not take the full step.

When you look at the world through the perception of the physical senses, you see a world made out of solid matter, and this matter appears very real to the senses. When you go to the deeper level of perception that was opened up by Einstein's findings, you see a different world, a world where matter has no reality or independent existence because everything is made out of energy—vibrations. When you go to the even deeper level of perceiving at the level of quantum physics, then you see that the world is not truly made out of energy. The world is made out of information, yet it does not end there.

A world made of information

There is an even deeper level of perception, for what is information? Does information have an existence independently of consciousness? Many people will immediately say that information can exist on its own. For example, they will say that the libraries of the world contain billions of books that store information. They will say that the world has millions of computers that store vast amounts of information on their hard drives and servers. Does a computer truly store *information,* or does it simply store *data?* Does a book store information, or does it simply store letters and numbers? Does the computer know what is stored on its hard drive? Does a book know what is stored on its pages?

What is in a book is not information—any more or any less than what is in a rock or a galaxy. One of the old Greek philosophers, named Pythagoras, said that everything is numbers. He might as well have said that everything is information.

What scientists have already proven is that there is information encoded in everything. What scientists are attempting to achieve is to decode the information in nature so they can understand why nature works the way it does and why it takes on the form that it does. This is the entire purpose of science—to decode the information that is stored in nature.

What is it that scientists are using in their attempts to decode this information? You might say they are using scientific instruments, but does a telescope really reveal information about a distant star? Or does the light rays passed on by the telescope become information only when they enter and are processed by a conscious mind?

When you open up your computer and the computer displays data on the screen, even the data on the screen is not information. It only becomes information when it enters your mind and is processed there by you attaching some meaning to what is otherwise meaningless data. What I have previously called curiosity is the desire for meaning, the desire to find patterns and meaning in everything you see around you in the material universe.

This is humankind's oldest quest. Where does this quest come from, where does this quest take place? It comes from a deep inner desire to know, a deep inner desire to find meaning. The quest itself takes place within the human mind!

Why is this so? It is so because the fundamental building block of everything that exists is consciousness. Everything is created out of consciousness. What you experience in yourself, as the drive to know and understand, is consciousness longing to experience itself through you.

What drives the quest for both a spiritual understanding and a rational, scientific understanding is the drive of consciousness to look at itself through you. This has some important ramifications that we will explore in the following chapter.

13 | THE RELATIONSHIP BETWEEN PEOPLE AND PLANET

Let us begin by looking at your experience as a human being on earth. You live at a very exciting time when humankind has made immense progress. It seems as if every day new discoveries are made, new forms of technology are developed. What drives this immense progress is that humankind has expanded its understanding of the world.

What is the basis for this expansion of understanding? From a superficial viewpoint you might say that it is information. Human beings today have infinitely more information about the material universe and how it works than the cavemen of only a few thousand years ago. It is true that information has driven progress, but as I have just explained, there is a deeper dimension. Where does information exist? It exists only in the human mind. It becomes useful only when processed by a human mind.

You may take all of the information discovered about the physical universe and encode it into a computer. You can get the computer to organize and manipulate this information in various ways, but you cannot get the computer to understand what this information means to a human mind. Even though people have made tremendous progress, this progress has been made only on one side of the coin of life.

Human beings, at least in the Western world, have so far ignored the other side of the coin of life. They have attempted to gather information about the material world, but they have not attempted to study the very instrument that allows them to gather and apply this information, namely the human mind.

If people would start studying the mind, then even more progress could be made than what you see today. What I am giving you here is an alternative to the worldview of both religion and materialistic science. What I am giving you is a vision that everything in the material universe, including planet earth, is made up through a process that has not yet been understood by either mainstream religion or science.

The formless source of all form

Let me give you a deeper description of this process. Let us begin by going beyond the material universe. The material universe exists in a certain spectrum of frequencies and there are energy frequencies beyond the material universe, namely a spiritual realm.

If you continue to go towards higher and higher frequencies, you would – from a logical, linear viewpoint – think you would end up at the ultimate frequency. This is both true and not true. There is a highest frequency in what we might call the "world of form," but this highest frequency is not the ultimate reality. For there to be a frequency, there must be a wave, and for there to be a wave, there must be something that can vibrate. A wave in the ocean propagates through the medium of water, a radio wave propagates through a medium, as does sound.

For there to be any kind of vibration, there must be some basic substance or reality that can be put into vibration. Where does this basic substance come from? If you go beyond the realm of what vibrates, you go into an entirely different realm that cannot be fathomed by the linear state of consciousness and cannot be described by the linear medium of words. This is nevertheless a state of consciousness. It is a unified, omnipresent state of awareness, which is what people for many thousands of years have been calling God, although most of the people who use the word "God" have not even begun to understand the state of consciousness I am talking about.

Any time you see people talk about a God and then apply some kind of linear form to that God, they have not understood the true nature of God. God is beyond anything that has form, anything that vibrates. When you go beyond the level of vibration, then you go into the pure awareness that is God. This is a self-aware being, which I would like to call the Creator.

This Creator is the source, the origin, of the entire world of form in which you live. This Creator is nothing like the Old Testament God, or the many other images of God found in religions around the world.

The Creator has no form; the Creator is the source of form. The Creator is a self-aware being with a state of consciousness – self-awareness – that is beyond what anyone on earth can even begin to fathom. You can use the mind's ability to get a glimpse of this state of awareness, and throughout the ages many people have had such mystical experiences.

The Creator is a self-aware being with a desire to create, to express itself. This is not something that was forced upon the Creator. It is driven by love, an unconditional form of love that wants to be expressed and that finds ultimate joy in expressing itself. The Creator created the world of form, in which you live, out of pure love, out of pure joy.

How the world was created

How did the Creator create the world of form? We have released other books that explains this in more detail (see *Cosmology of Evil*), but I will give a brief summary here. In the Creator's self-awareness there can be no distinction, no separation. It is not possible for the Creator to create something that has a distinct or separate form. In order to create anything, the Creator must begin by creating a void in which forms can exist and appear to be separate. The Creator withdrew its own Being, its own Presence, and created a space, a void.

The Creator then created a sphere in the center of this void. This sphere was created out of the basic substance of creation, which is what I, in another book [*A Course in Abundance*] have called the Ma-ter Light. This is a substance that cannot be detected by any material instrument for the simple reason that it has no form. It does not even have vibration, but it has the potential to be stirred into vibrations. If you want a linear illustration – which, of course, can only be inaccurate – then consider the ocean when it is completely still and without any waves. This ocean can be said to have no waves, but when a wind starts blowing, then the ocean can be stirred into waves.

This Ma-ter Light is not something that exists separately from or independently of the Creator. The Creator fashions the Ma-ter Light out of its own Being, out of its own consciousness. At the level of the Creator, there is nothing but consciousness.

After having created the initial sphere and having created certain structures, certain forms, within that sphere, the Creator then projected extensions of itself into that sphere. These extensions took on the form of individual beings with a localized sense of self-awareness. This is in contrast to the Creator, which has an omnipresent, non-localized sense of self-awareness. The Creator is able to look at its creation from every single point at the same time, but it cannot look at its creation from one single point exclusively. It attained this capability only by creating extensions of itself that appear as individual beings that look at the world of form from a particular, localized vantage point.

After this initial sphere was created, the self-aware extensions of the Creator began the process of expanding their sense of self-awareness. Their goal was to no longer see themselves as localized beings but to become aware of themselves as extensions of the omnipresent Creator. When they had attained that level of self-awareness, their entire sphere was raised to a higher level of vibration. Their entire sphere ascended and now became part of what you today – from your vantage point – see as the spiritual realm.

The purpose of life is to raise self-awareness

The initial sphere was not the only sphere. There have been several of these spheres, and your material universe is part of the latest of these, which is the seventh in number. The latest sphere in which you find yourself has not yet reached the ascension point. There are not enough beings within it who have reached the level of self-awareness where they see themselves as extensions of the Creator. The purpose for the entire world of form is not, as traditional religion might have it, that the Creator desires to be worshiped and admired. The deeper purpose is that each self-aware extension of the Creator has the potential to expand its self-awareness until it reaches the same level of awareness as the Creator.

In the New Testament there is a situation where Jesus is accused of blasphemy. He refers to a statement from the Old Testament, which says: "Ye are gods." The reality is that each human being is a God in the making. Regardless of the level of self-awareness you have today, you have the potential to expand your self-awareness and to continue to do so.

The first threshold that will be passed for you is when you reach the level of the ascension. You can ascend from the material realm and become an ascended, immortal being in the spiritual realm that is right above the material universe in vibration. From there you can continue to grow through all of the previous spheres, until you reach the highest of these spheres. Then you can cross another threshold and attain the self-awareness of a Creator. Thereby, you become able to create your own world of form, your own universe. This is the purpose of life, the purpose of creation: the growth in self-awareness.

What has happened on earth – from the caveman stage to the present civilization – is that there has been a growth in self-awareness. This growth could take a quantum leap if the people who are ready – and who have taken embodiment for this purpose – would become more aware of the potential of the human mind.

Everything is created out of one basic substance that I call the Ma-ter Light. This Ma-ter Light has the potential to take on any form, yet it cannot take on form by itself. It takes on form when a self-aware being envisions at particular form and then projects that form onto the Ma-ter Light.

13 | The Relationship Between People and Planet

I said that the so-called miracles performed by Jesus were not miracles but the application of a higher natural law. When you reach a certain level of self-awareness, you become able to activate this natural law. You will be able to consciously formulate an image and deliberately project it onto the Ma-ter Light whereby you will instantly see the Ma-ter Light conform to the image and thereby manifest the form that you envisioned.

When Jesus looked at a man with a withered hand, his consciousness did not see what the consciousness of most human beings would have seen. He did not see a withered hand; he did not see any imperfect state as real or permanent. Jesus saw beyond the outer form of the withered hand. He saw that the withered hand was made up of a basic substance that had only temporarily taken on the form of the withered hand. Jesus also saw that this substance, this Ma-ter Light, could as easily take on the form of a perfectly healthy hand as the form that it had temporarily taken on.

Jesus saw that the withered hand was simply a manifestation of the man's imperfect and unbalanced state of consciousness. Jesus held the vision for a healthy hand, and he superimposed that vision upon the Ma-ter Light that made up the withered hand. Because Jesus' consciousness was so much higher than the consciousness of the man with the withered hand, Jesus' consciousness could override the other man's consciousness and instantly heal the hand.

Be careful to realize that there were people who sought healing from Jesus but Jesus did not heal them. The reason is that Jesus did not come to do everything for everyone; he came to show people what they have the power to do by developing the same state of consciousness that Jesus had attained. He only performed certain healings as a demonstration of what was possible. It was the intention that people should use this to develop the powers of their own minds, instead of looking to

Jesus to do it all for them. This is the shift that needs to happen among the spiritual and open-minded people in today's world. If you are truly concerned about planet earth and the future of planet earth, then the most important thing you can do is to begin to expand your understanding of the human mind and its true potential.

All material conditions can be changed

You may, right now, look at environmental problems or natural disasters and think you are powerless to change them. This is because you are looking at these problems through the filter of the same state of consciousness that created them. That state of consciousness is very much focused on the material world, and it tends to see material conditions as real. To this state of consciousness material conditions form a real limitation, a real boundary, for human capabilities. Once you raise your consciousness beyond that level, you begin to glimpse – gradually and over time – that there is a deeper understanding of life.

Matter is not truly as real as it appears to the senses and a certain level of awareness. Once you begin to realize that matter is not ultimately real, then you also begin to accept that matter does not form an impenetrable boundary. Matter is not beyond change.

You may look at planet earth today and you may think that pollution or global warming has gone beyond a threshold from which there is no way back, and things can only get worse. Once you raise your awareness, you see that every condition that could possibly exist in a physical form can be changed by applying a higher vision. Once you begin to realize that every physical form is the outpicturing of information that has been applied to the basic substance of the Ma-ter Light, you realize that any physical form can be changed by applying different information to that same Ma-ter Light.

Comparing the world to a computer

This is not unlike what you have experienced when working on a computer. You know that what appears as images on your computer screen does not have an ultimate reality. You can, in various ways, change the appearance of any image on your computer screen. How is this accomplished?

The image on the computer screen is made up entirely of information. On the computer's hard drive or in its memory, the image you see does not exist; there are only "zeros" and "ones" arranged in different sequences. By applying a different sequence, a different form of information, you can change the image on the computer screen and you can do so instantly. The computer screen has the capability to display any image you can imagine, but of course it cannot imagine images on its own. It can only outpicture what you apply to it.

This is the same with Mother Earth. This planet has the potential to outpicture the abundant life and a completely balanced state of nature. The current imbalances – in the form of natural disasters, pollution or the lack of resources or food – are brought about because the earth is outpicturing the imbalances in the collective consciousness of humankind. If a critical mass of people will attain a higher vision – and use the powers of their minds to superimpose that vision upon the physical planet – then you will begin to see changes.

Take note that I am not hereby saying that those who are concerned about the future of Mother Earth should not take physical actions. I am not trying to say that you should sit in a cave in the Himalayas and meditate all day and that you should withdraw from society. On the contrary, it is not my intention here to say that people who have been engaged in the environmental issue or social or political issues should withdraw.

It is my intention to say that if you will make an effort to raise your level of consciousness, you will find that you will gradually begin to attain a new understanding, a new vision, of the problems that you today might see as being beyond change. You will gain a new foundation for engaging yourself in society. You will become one of the forerunners for taking the debate in society to a new and higher level where people will begin to see solutions that they cannot see today.

There was a time when people had not discovered bacteria, and therefore many diseases seemed incurable. With the simple discovery of bacteria as the cause of many diseases, there was – instantly – a shift in the debate around health. Suddenly, people could see ways to cure diseases that had not been seen before. If the environmental debate, and the general debate in society, could be lifted to a higher level, then people would begin to find ways to combat pollution and global warming that simply cannot be seen today.

It is not that the solutions are not there; it is simply that they have not been discovered. The reason they have not been discovered is that so far the debate has been centered on superficial conditions that are not the real cause. If the debate was to be expanded to include the deeper causes, then the solutions would become apparent.

14 | USING THE INVOCATIONS

In the following chapters you will find four invocations that are designed to consume fear-based energy in the four octaves: physical, emotional, mental and identity. You read the invocations aloud, as described earlier in the book.

You can use these invocations in various ways, depending on how much time you have. It takes 15-20 minutes to give one invocation (depending on your speed). Here are a few suggestions for how you can use the invocations for a more organized vigil:

• Give the first invocation once a day for nine days. Then give the second invocation once a day for nine days an so on with the third and fourth invocation.

• If you can spend more time, give two invocations a day for nine days and then move on to the other two.

- Give one or two invocations a day for 33 days. Then move on to the following invocations.

- If you can spend an hour a day, give all four invocations every day for nine or 33 days.

If you are unsure how to get started, you can purchase recordings of the invocations on *www.morepublish.com*. The recordings come as mp3 files that you can download and use on your computer or music player.

Also remember that there are many other invocations available for free at *www.transcendencetoolbox.com*. These cover a wide range of topics from personal growth to world conditions. You can also find additional invocations that are available in some of the other books released by the ascended masters. There are currently over 150 invocations and that number will go up in the future. No matter what your field of interest might be, there is likely to be one or more invocations that will help you invoke light into the area of society where you would like to see change.

15 | INVOKING LIGHT INTO THE PHYSICAL OCTAVE

In the name of the I AM THAT I AM, the One Mind within me and within all life, I call upon Archangel Michael to take command over the physical octave on earth and clear it of all fear-based energies in accordance with the vision of Christ. I call for Mother Mary to flood the physical octave with the Mother Flame and consume all that is anti-love. I call for Saint Germain to flood the earth with an irresistible surge of Violet Flame to transmute all fear-based energies. I especially call for Archangel Michael, Mother Mary and Saint Germain to take command over …

[Make your own calls here.]

Part 1

1. Archangel Michael, I am willing to experience your Flaming Presence so that I can know that your energies can protect myself and all constructive people from fear-based energies.

> Archangel Michael, light so blue,
> my heart has room for only you.
> My mind is one, no longer two,
> your love for me is ever true.
>
> **Archangel Michael, you are here,**
> **your light consumes all doubt and fear.**
> **Your Presence is forever near,**
> **you are to me so very dear.**

2. Archangel Michael, place a shield of blue-flame protection around my four lower bodies and those of all constructive people. Seal us from all fear-based energies and the people or forces using such energies to block our Divine plans.

> Archangel Michael, I will be,
> all one with your reality.
> No fear can hold me as I see,
> this world no power has o'er me.
>
> **Archangel Michael, you are here,**
> **your light consumes all doubt and fear.**
> **Your Presence is forever near,**
> **you are to me so very dear.**

3. Archangel Michael, consume all fear-based energies that create downward spirals of conflict between various groups of people, even entire nations.

> Archangel Michael, hold me tight,
> shatter now the darkest night.
> Clear my chakras with your light,
> restore to me my inner sight.
>
> **Archangel Michael, you are here,**
> **your light consumes all doubt and fear.**
> **Your Presence is forever near,**
> **you are to me so very dear.**

4. Archangel Michael, consume all fear-based energies that block communication, understanding and mutual respect among people.

> Archangel Michael, now I stand,
> with you the light I do command.
> My heart I ever will expand,
> till highest truth I understand.
>
> **Archangel Michael, you are here,**
> **your light consumes all doubt and fear.**
> **Your Presence is forever near,**
> **you are to me so very dear.**

5. Archangel Michael, consume all fear-based energies that create downward spirals of war. Consume the energetic records of all past wars.

Archangel Michael, in my heart,
from me you never will depart.
Of hierarchy I am a part,
I now accept a fresh new start.

**Archangel Michael, you are here,
your light consumes all doubt and fear.
Your Presence is forever near,
you are to me so very dear.**

6. Archangel Michael, consume all fear-based energies in the downward spirals that allow a small elite to abuse power and control the population. Expose this power elite and their manipulation for all to see.

Archangel Michael, sword of blue,
all darkness you are cutting through.
My Christhood I do now pursue,
discernment shows me what is true.

**Archangel Michael, you are here,
your light consumes all doubt and fear.
Your Presence is forever near,
you are to me so very dear.**

7. Archangel Michael, consume all fear-based energies in the downward spirals that allow a small elite to manipulate the economies and money systems of nations and the world.

Archangel Michael, in your wings,
I now let go of lesser things.
God's homing call in my heart rings,
my heart with yours forever sings.

**Archangel Michael, you are here,
your light consumes all doubt and fear.
Your Presence is forever near,
you are to me so very dear.**

8. Archangel Michael, consume all fear-based energies in the downward spirals that allow a small elite to keep the majority of the world's population living beneath the poverty level.

Archangel Michael, take me home,
in higher spheres I want to roam.
I am reborn from cosmic foam,
my life is now a sacred poem.

**Archangel Michael, you are here,
your light consumes all doubt and fear.
Your Presence is forever near,
you are to me so very dear.**

9. Archangel Michael, consume all fear-based energies in the downward spirals that allow a small elite to use both scientific materialism and religion to keep people ignorant of the spiritual dynamic on earth.

Archangel Michael, light you are,
shining like the bluest star.
You are a cosmic avatar,
with you I will go very far.

**Archangel Michael, you are here,
your light consumes all doubt and fear.
Your Presence is forever near,
you are to me so very dear.**

Part 2

1. Archangel Michael, consume all fear-based energies in the downward spirals that cause imbalances in the physical planet, leading to earthquakes.

> Archangel Michael, light so blue,
> my heart has room for only you.
> My mind is one, no longer two,
> your love for me is ever true.
>
> **Archangel Michael, you are here,**
> **your light consumes all doubt and fear.**
> **Your Presence is forever near,**
> **you are to me so very dear.**

2. Archangel Michael, consume all fear-based energies in the downward spirals that cause imbalances in the physical planet, leading to volcanic eruptions.

> Archangel Michael, I will be,
> all one with your reality.
> No fear can hold me as I see,
> this world no power has o'er me.
>
> **Archangel Michael, you are here,**
> **your light consumes all doubt and fear.**
> **Your Presence is forever near,**
> **you are to me so very dear.**

3. Archangel Michael, consume all fear-based energies in the downward spirals that cause imbalances in the physical planet, leading to extreme weather patterns.

> Archangel Michael, hold me tight,
> shatter now the darkest night.
> Clear my chakras with your light,
> restore to me my inner sight.

> **Archangel Michael, you are here,**
> **your light consumes all doubt and fear.**
> **Your Presence is forever near,**
> **you are to me so very dear.**

4. Archangel Michael, consume all fear-based energies in the downward spirals that cause imbalances in the physical planet, leading to a lack of natural resources.

> Archangel Michael, now I stand,
> with you the light I do command.
> My heart I ever will expand,
> till highest truth I understand.

> **Archangel Michael, you are here,**
> **your light consumes all doubt and fear.**
> **Your Presence is forever near,**
> **you are to me so very dear.**

5. Archangel Michael, consume all fear-based energies in the downward spirals that cause imbalances in the physical planet, leading to a decrease in people's lifespan.

Archangel Michael, in my heart,
from me you never will depart.
Of hierarchy I am a part,
I now accept a fresh new start.

**Archangel Michael, you are here,
your light consumes all doubt and fear.
Your Presence is forever near,
you are to me so very dear.**

6. Archangel Michael, consume all fear-based energies in the downward spirals that cause imbalances in the physical planet, leading to diseases that prevent people from fulfilling their Divine plans.

Archangel Michael, sword of blue,
all darkness you are cutting through.
My Christhood I do now pursue,
discernment shows me what is true.

**Archangel Michael, you are here,
your light consumes all doubt and fear.
Your Presence is forever near,
you are to me so very dear.**

7. Archangel Michael, consume all fear-based energies in the downward spirals that cause imbalances in the physical planet, as a result of man-made pollution.

Archangel Michael, in your wings,
I now let go of lesser things.
God's homing call in my heart rings,
my heart with yours forever sings.

**Archangel Michael, you are here,
your light consumes all doubt and fear.
Your Presence is forever near,
you are to me so very dear.**

8. Archangel Michael, consume all fear-based energies in the downward spirals that cause imbalances in the physical planet, as a result of the power elite's desire for profit at all cost.

Archangel Michael, take me home,
in higher spheres I want to roam.
I am reborn from cosmic foam,
my life is now a sacred poem.

**Archangel Michael, you are here,
your light consumes all doubt and fear.
Your Presence is forever near,
you are to me so very dear.**

9. Archangel Michael, consume all fear-based energies in the downward spirals that cause imbalances in the physical planet, as a result of people's ignorance of how the earth responds to our consciousness.

Archangel Michael, light you are,
shining like the bluest star.
You are a cosmic avatar,
with you I will go very far.

**Archangel Michael, you are here,
your light consumes all doubt and fear.
Your Presence is forever near,
you are to me so very dear.**

Part 3

1. Mother Mary, send the Mother Flame to consume the fear-based energies that prevent people from acknowledging that everything on earth is created from consciousness and responds to our consciousness.

> O blessed Mary, Mother mine,
> there is no greater love than thine,
> as we are one in heart and mind,
> my place in hierarchy I find.
>
> **O Mother Mary, generate,**
> **the song that does accelerate,**
> **the earth into a higher state,**
> **all matter does now scintillate.**

2. Mother Mary, send the Mother Flame to consume the fear-based energies that prevent people from acknowledging that we have collectively created all of the limiting conditions we face on this planet and that only we can uncreate them.

> I came to earth from heaven sent,
> as I am in embodiment,
> I use Divine authority,
> commanding you to set earth free.
>
> **O Mother Mary, generate,**
> **the song that does accelerate,**
> **the earth into a higher state,**
> **all matter does now scintillate.**

3. Mother Mary, send the Mother Flame to consume the fear-based energies that prevent people from acknowledging that the earth has been inhabited for a very long time and that humankind has generated enormous amounts of fear-based energy spirals.

> I call now in God's sacred name,
> for you to use your Mother Flame,
> to burn all fear-based energy,
> restoring sacred harmony.

O Mother Mary, generate,
the song that does accelerate,
the earth into a higher state,
all matter does now scintillate.

4. Mother Mary, send the Mother Flame to consume the fear-based energies that prevent people from acknowledging that we have been lead into doing this by a small power elite of beings who want to control us for selfish purposes.

> Your sacred name I hereby praise,
> collective consciousness you raise,
> no more of fear and doubt and shame,
> consume it with your Mother Flame.

O Mother Mary, generate,
the song that does accelerate,
the earth into a higher state,
all matter does now scintillate.

5. Mother Mary, send the Mother Flame to consume the fear-based energies that prevent people from acknowledging that we have a right to stand up against this power elite and demand that they be removed from the earth by the ascended masters.

All darkness from the earth you purge,
your light moves as a mighty surge,
no force of darkness can now stop,
the spiral that goes only up.

**O Mother Mary, generate,
the song that does accelerate,
the earth into a higher state,
all matter does now scintillate.**

6. Mother Mary, send the Mother Flame to consume the fear-based energies that prevent people from acknowledging that we must take responsibility for our planet and work with the ascended masters to escape the control of the power elite.

All elemental life you bless,
removing from them man-made stress,
the nature spirits are now free,
outpicturing Divine decree.

**O Mother Mary, generate,
the song that does accelerate,
the earth into a higher state,
all matter does now scintillate.**

7. Mother Mary, send the Mother Flame to consume the fear-based energies that prevent people from acknowledging that the ascended masters have a plan for removing war, disease and poverty from this planet.

> I raise my voice and take my stand,
> a stop to war I do command,
> no more shall warring scar the earth,
> a golden age is given birth.

> **O Mother Mary, generate,**
> **the song that does accelerate,**
> **the earth into a higher state,**
> **all matter does now scintillate.**

8. Mother Mary, send the Mother Flame to consume the fear-based energies that prevent people from acknowledging that the earth has the potential to give us a far more abundant life than what we see manifest right now.

> As Mother Earth is free at last,
> disasters belong to the past,
> your Mother Light is so intense,
> that matter is now far less dense.

> **O Mother Mary, generate,**
> **the song that does accelerate,**
> **the earth into a higher state,**
> **all matter does now scintillate.**

9. Mother Mary, send the Mother Flame to consume the fear-based energies that prevent people from acknowledging that we can manifest the abundant life on earth only by accepting our roles as co-creators.

> In Mother Light the earth is pure,
> the upward spiral will endure,
> prosperity is now the norm,
> God's vision manifest as form.
>
> **O Mother Mary, generate,**
> **the song that does accelerate,**
> **the earth into a higher state,**
> **all matter does now scintillate.**

Part 4

1. Saint Germain, send flood tides of Violet Flame to consume the karmic vulnerability of myself and all constructive people to any kind of physical misfortune, especially so-called natural disasters.

> O Saint Germain, you do inspire,
> my vision raised forever higher,
> with you I form a figure-eight,
> your Golden Age I co-create.
>
> **O Saint Germain, what love you bring,**
> **it truly makes all matter sing,**
> **your violet flame does all restore,**
> **with you we are becoming more.**

2. Saint Germain, send flood tides of Violet Flame to consume the karmic vulnerability of myself and all constructive people to any kind of physical misfortune, especially violence and crime.

> O Saint Germain, what Freedom Flame,
> released when we recite your name,
> acceleration is your gift,
> our planet it will surely lift.
>
> **O Saint Germain, what love you bring,**
> **it truly makes all matter sing,**
> **your violet flame does all restore,**
> **with you we are becoming more.**

3. Saint Germain, send flood tides of Violet Flame to consume the karmic vulnerability of myself and all constructive people to any kind of physical misfortune, especially conflict and war.

> O Saint Germain, in love we claim,
> our right to bring your violet flame,
> from you Above, to us below,
> it is an all-transforming flow.
>
> **O Saint Germain, what love you bring,**
> **it truly makes all matter sing,**
> **your violet flame does all restore,**
> **with you we are becoming more.**

4. Saint Germain, send flood tides of Violet Flame to consume the karmic vulnerability of myself and all constructive people to any kind of physical misfortune, especially disease.

O Saint Germain, I love you so,
my aura filled with violet glow,
my chakras filled with violet fire,
I am your cosmic amplifier.

**O Saint Germain, what love you bring,
it truly makes all matter sing,
your violet flame does all restore,
with you we are becoming more.**

5. Saint Germain, send flood tides of Violet Flame to consume the karmic vulnerability of myself and all constructive people to poverty and other financial burdens.

O Saint Germain, I am now free,
your violet flame is therapy,
transform all hang-ups in my mind,
as inner peace I surely find.

**O Saint Germain, what love you bring,
it truly makes all matter sing,
your violet flame does all restore,
with you we are becoming more.**

6. Saint Germain, send flood tides of Violet Flame to transmute the fear-based energies that prevent the constructive people from seeing their Divine plans and accepting their potential to bring positive change.

O Saint Germain, my body pure,
your violet flame for all is cure,
consume the cause of all disease,
and therefore I am all at ease.

**O Saint Germain, what love you bring,
it truly makes all matter sing,
your violet flame does all restore,
with you we are becoming more.**

7. Saint Germain, send flood tides of Violet Flame to transmute all fear-based energy that blocks the emergence of new political ideas and technology that will eradicate poverty and disease.

O Saint Germain, I'm karma-free,
the past no longer burdens me,
a brand new opportunity,
I am in Christic unity.

**O Saint Germain, what love you bring,
it truly makes all matter sing,
your violet flame does all restore,
with you we are becoming more.**

8. Saint Germain, send flood tides of Violet Flame to transmute all fear-based energy that prevents the constructive people from seeing the matrix for your golden age and their personal role in manifesting it.

O Saint Germain, we are now one,
I am for you a violet sun,
as we transform this planet earth,
your Golden Age is given birth.

> **O Saint Germain, what love you bring,**
> **it truly makes all matter sing,**
> **your violet flame does all restore,**
> **with you we are becoming more.**

9. Saint Germain, send flood tides of Violet Flame to transmute all fear-based energy that prevents a wide-scale spiritual awakening that causes millions of people to recognize the ascended masters and use their teachings and tools to change the world.

> O Saint Germain, the earth is free,
> from burden of duality,
> in oneness we bring what is best,
> your Golden Age is manifest.

> **O Saint Germain, what love you bring,**
> **it truly makes all matter sing,**
> **your violet flame does all restore,**
> **with you we are becoming more.**

Sealing

In the name of the I AM THAT I AM, the One Mind within me and within all life, I accept that Archangel Michael, Astrea and Shiva form an impenetrable shield around myself and all constructive people on earth, sealing us from all fear-based energies in all four octaves. I accept that the Light of God is consuming and transforming all fear-based energies on earth!

16 | INVOKING LIGHT INTO THE EMOTIONAL OCTAVE

In the name of the I AM THAT I AM, the One Mind within me and within all life, I call upon Shiva to take command over the emotional octave on earth and consume all fear-based energy spirals in accordance with the vision of Christ. I call for Mother Mary to heal the emotional wounds of all constructive people. I call for Saint Germain to flood the emotional octave with an irresistible surge of Violet Flame to transmute all energies that block the creative flow through the emotional octave. I especially call for Shiva, Mother Mary and Saint Germain to take command over …

[Make your own calls here.]

Part 1

1. Beloved Shiva, use your unlimited Sacred Fire to consume all fear-based energies that block the Divine plan of myself and all constructive people

> O Shiva, God of Sacred Fire,
> It's time to let the past expire,
> I want to rise above the old,
> a golden future to unfold.
>
> **O Shiva, clear the energy,**
> **O Shiva, bring the synergy,**
> **O Shiva, make all demons flee,**
> **O Shiva, bring back peace to me.**

2. Beloved Shiva, consume all fear-based energies that stir up the emotional bodies of myself and all constructive people, preventing us from being in control of our emotional reactions.

> O Shiva, come and set me free,
> from forces that do limit me,
> with fire consume all that is less,
> paving way for my success.
>
> **O Shiva, clear the energy,**
> **O Shiva, bring the synergy,**
> **O Shiva, make all demons flee,**
> **O Shiva, bring back peace to me.**

3. Beloved Shiva, consume all fear-based energies that block the free flow of creative energies through the emotional bodies of myself and all constructive people.

> O Shiva, Maya's veil disperse,
> clear my private universe,
> dispel the consciousness of death,
> consume it with your Sacred Breath.

> **O Shiva, clear the energy,**
> **O Shiva, bring the synergy,**
> **O Shiva, make all demons flee,**
> **O Shiva, bring back peace to me.**

4. Beloved Shiva, cut free myself and all constructive people from the emotional attachments that make us vulnerable to being overpowered by the planetary spirals of fear-based emotional energies.

> O Shiva, I hereby let go,
> of all attachments here below,
> addictive entities consume,
> the upward path I do resume.

> **O Shiva, clear the energy,**
> **O Shiva, bring the synergy,**
> **O Shiva, make all demons flee,**
> **O Shiva, bring back peace to me.**

5. Beloved Shiva, cut free myself and all constructive people from the emotional wounds that make us vulnerable to being manipulated by the power elite and the dark forces behind them.

O Shiva, I recite your name,
come banish fear and doubt and shame,
with fire expose within my mind,
what ego seeks to hide behind.

O Shiva, clear the energy,
O Shiva, bring the synergy,
O Shiva, make all demons flee,
O Shiva, bring back peace to me.

6. Beloved Shiva, cut free myself and all constructive people from the raw fear that makes us afraid to take a stand against the power elite and demand change on this planet.

O Shiva, I am not afraid,
my karmic debt hereby is paid,
the past no longer owns my choice,
in breath of Shiva I rejoice.

O Shiva, clear the energy,
O Shiva, bring the synergy,
O Shiva, make all demons flee,
O Shiva, bring back peace to me.

7. Beloved Shiva, cut free myself and all constructive people from the emotional scars that cause such imbalances that we cannot fulfill our Divine plans

O Shiva, show me spirit pairs,
that keep me trapped in their affairs,
I choose to see within my mind,
the spirits that you surely bind.

**O Shiva, clear the energy,
O Shiva, bring the synergy,
O Shiva, make all demons flee,
O Shiva, bring back peace to me.**

8. Beloved Shiva, cut free myself and all constructive people from the emotional energy that causes us to be so trapped in personal conflicts that we cannot fulfill our Divine plans.

O Shiva, naked I now stand,
my mind in freedom does expand,
as all my ghosts I do release,
surrender is the key to peace.

**O Shiva, clear the energy,
O Shiva, bring the synergy,
O Shiva, make all demons flee,
O Shiva, bring back peace to me.**

9. Beloved Shiva, cut free myself and all constructive people from the emotional trap of feeling unworthy to serve the cause of bringing a golden age to earth.

O Shiva, all-consuming fire,
with Parvati raise me higher,
when I am raised your light to see,
all men I will draw onto me.

**O Shiva, clear the energy,
O Shiva, bring the synergy,
O Shiva, make all demons flee,
O Shiva, bring back peace to me.**

Part 2

1. Beloved Shiva, consume the spirals of fear-based energies, the power elite and the dark forces that seek to prevent us from making a difference by getting us involved with never-ending spirals of conflict and war.

> O Shiva, God of Sacred Fire,
> It's time to let the past expire,
> I want to rise above the old,
> a golden future to unfold.
>
> **O Shiva, clear the energy,**
> **O Shiva, bring the synergy,**
> **O Shiva, make all demons flee,**
> **O Shiva, bring back peace to me.**

2. Beloved Shiva, consume the spirals of fear-based energies, the power elite and the dark forces that seek to prevent us from making a difference by keeping us ignorant of their own existence and the existence of the ascended masters.

> O Shiva, come and set me free,
> from forces that do limit me,
> with fire consume all that is less,
> paving way for my success.
>
> **O Shiva, clear the energy,**
> **O Shiva, bring the synergy,**
> **O Shiva, make all demons flee,**
> **O Shiva, bring back peace to me.**

3. Beloved Shiva, consume the spirals of fear-based energies, the power elite and the dark forces that seek to prevent us from making a difference by keeping us trapped in poverty or the pursuit of material possessions.

> O Shiva, Maya's veil disperse,
> clear my private universe,
> dispel the consciousness of death,
> consume it with your Sacred Breath.

> **O Shiva, clear the energy,**
> **O Shiva, bring the synergy,**
> **O Shiva, make all demons flee,**
> **O Shiva, bring back peace to me.**

4. Beloved Shiva, consume the spirals of fear-based energies, the power elite and the dark forces that seek to prevent us from making a difference by keeping us trapped in physical and emotional diseases.

> O Shiva, I hereby let go,
> of all attachments here below,
> addictive entities consume,
> the upward path I do resume.

> **O Shiva, clear the energy,**
> **O Shiva, bring the synergy,**
> **O Shiva, make all demons flee,**
> **O Shiva, bring back peace to me.**

5. Beloved Shiva, consume the spirals of fear-based energies, the power elite and the dark forces that seek to prevent us from making a difference by keeping us trapped in feeling inferior and unworthy or pursuing superiority on earth.

> O Shiva, I recite your name,
> come banish fear and doubt and shame,
> with fire expose within my mind,
> what ego seeks to hide behind.
>
> **O Shiva, clear the energy,**
> **O Shiva, bring the synergy,**
> **O Shiva, make all demons flee,**
> **O Shiva, bring back peace to me.**

6. Beloved Shiva, consume the spirals of fear-based energies, the power elite and the dark forces that seek to prevent us from making a difference by blocking our awareness of how we have co-created the limitations we face.

> O Shiva, I am not afraid,
> my karmic debt hereby is paid,
> the past no longer owns my choice,
> in breath of Shiva I rejoice.
>
> **O Shiva, clear the energy,**
> **O Shiva, bring the synergy,**
> **O Shiva, make all demons flee,**
> **O Shiva, bring back peace to me.**

7. Beloved Shiva, consume the spirals of fear-based energies, the power elite and the dark forces that seek to prevent us from making a difference by making us believe we do not have the responsibility or the ability to change the world.

> O Shiva, show me spirit pairs,
> that keep me trapped in their affairs,
> I choose to see within my mind,
> the spirits that you surely bind.

> **O Shiva, clear the energy,**
> **O Shiva, bring the synergy,**
> **O Shiva, make all demons flee,**
> **O Shiva, bring back peace to me.**

8. Beloved Shiva, consume the spirals of fear-based energies, the power elite and the dark forces that seek to prevent us from making a difference by blaming God for current conditions.

> O Shiva, naked I now stand,
> my mind in freedom does expand,
> as all my ghosts I do release,
> surrender is the key to peace.

> **O Shiva, clear the energy,**
> **O Shiva, bring the synergy,**
> **O Shiva, make all demons flee,**
> **O Shiva, bring back peace to me.**

9. Beloved Shiva, consume the spirals of fear-based energies, the power elite and the dark forces that seek to prevent us from making a difference by keeping us focused on the material side of life.

O Shiva, all-consuming fire,
with Parvati raise me higher,
when I am raised your light to see,
all men I will draw onto me.

**O Shiva, clear the energy,
O Shiva, bring the synergy,
O Shiva, make all demons flee,
O Shiva, bring back peace to me.**

Part 3

1. Mother Mary, send the Mother Flame into the energy vortexes in the collective emotional body that cause people to be trapped in the illusion that the end can justify the means and that a worthy cause can justify violence.

O blessed Mary, Mother mine,
there is no greater love than thine,
as we are one in heart and mind,
my place in hierarchy I find.

**O Mother Mary, generate,
the song that does accelerate,
the earth into a higher state,
all matter does now scintillate.**

2. Mother Mary, send the Mother Flame into the energy vortexes in the collective emotional body that cause people to be trapped in the illusion that the only way to bring peace is to kill the people who will not submit to your control

16 | Invoking Light Into the Emotional Octave

I came to earth from heaven sent,
as I am in embodiment,
I use Divine authority,
commanding you to set earth free.

**O Mother Mary, generate,
the song that does accelerate,
the earth into a higher state,
all matter does now scintillate.**

3. Mother Mary, send the Mother Flame into the energy vortexes in the collective emotional body that cause people to be trapped in the illusion that there is only a limited amount of resources and wealth.

I call now in God's sacred name,
for you to use your Mother Flame,
to burn all fear-based energy,
restoring sacred harmony.

**O Mother Mary, generate,
the song that does accelerate,
the earth into a higher state,
all matter does now scintillate.**

4. Mother Mary, send the Mother Flame into the energy vortexes in the collective emotional body that cause people to be trapped in the illusion that the only way to get what you want is to take it from others through force.

Your sacred name I hereby praise,
collective consciousness you raise,
no more of fear and doubt and shame,
consume it with your Mother Flame.

O Mother Mary, generate,
the song that does accelerate,
the earth into a higher state,
all matter does now scintillate.

5. Mother Mary, send the Mother Flame into the energy vortexes in the collective emotional body that cause people to be trapped in the illusion that the use of force is inevitable or justified.

All darkness from the earth you purge,
your light moves as a mighty surge,
no force of darkness can now stop,
the spiral that goes only up.

O Mother Mary, generate,
the song that does accelerate,
the earth into a higher state,
all matter does now scintillate.

6. Mother Mary, send the Mother Flame into the energy vortexes in the collective emotional body that cause people to be trapped in the illusion that we must force Mother Nature to give us what we need.

16 | Invoking Light Into the Emotional Octave

All elemental life you bless,
removing from them man-made stress,
the nature spirits are now free,
outpicturing Divine decree.

**O Mother Mary, generate,
the song that does accelerate,
the earth into a higher state,
all matter does now scintillate.**

7. Mother Mary, send the Mother Flame into the energy vortexes in the collective emotional body that cause people to be trapped in the illusion that Mother Nature is unconscious and does not respond to our consciousness.

I raise my voice and take my stand,
a stop to war I do command,
no more shall warring scar the earth,
a golden age is given birth.

**O Mother Mary, generate,
the song that does accelerate,
the earth into a higher state,
all matter does now scintillate.**

8. Mother Mary, send the Mother Flame into the energy vortexes in the collective emotional body that prevent people from seeing that Mother Nature can as easily outpicture the abundant life as the current state of limitation.

As Mother Earth is free at last,
disasters belong to the past,
your Mother Light is so intense,
that matter is now far less dense.

**O Mother Mary, generate,
the song that does accelerate,
the earth into a higher state,
all matter does now scintillate.**

9. Mother Mary, send the Mother Flame into the energy vortexes in the collective emotional body that prevent people from seeing that Mother Nature can only outpicture what we project upon her through our individual minds and the collective mind.

In Mother Light the earth is pure,
the upward spiral will endure,
prosperity is now the norm,
God's vision manifest as form.

**O Mother Mary, generate,
the song that does accelerate,
the earth into a higher state,
all matter does now scintillate.**

Part 4

1. Saint Germain, send flood tides of Violet Flame to transmute the fear-based energies that pollute the higher levels of the emotional octave.

16 | Invoking Light Into the Emotional Octave

O Saint Germain, you do inspire,
my vision raised forever higher,
with you I form a figure-eight,
your Golden Age I co-create.

**O Saint Germain, what love you bring,
it truly makes all matter sing,
your violet flame does all restore,
with you we are becoming more.**

2. Saint Germain, send flood tides of Violet Flame to open the full flow of creative energies through the emotional octave.

O Saint Germain, what Freedom Flame,
released when we recite your name,
acceleration is your gift,
our planet it will surely lift.

**O Saint Germain, what love you bring,
it truly makes all matter sing,
your violet flame does all restore,
with you we are becoming more.**

3. Saint Germain, send flood tides of Violet Flame to clear out the fear-based emotional vortexes that produce warfare and conflict.

O Saint Germain, in love we claim,
our right to bring your violet flame,
from you Above, to us below,
it is an all-transforming flow.

**O Saint Germain, what love you bring,
it truly makes all matter sing,
your violet flame does all restore,
with you we are becoming more.**

4. Saint Germain, send flood tides of Violet Flame to clear out the fear-based emotional vortexes that produce all forms of discrimination, especially against women.

O Saint Germain, I love you so,
my aura filled with violet glow,
my chakras filled with violet fire,
I am your cosmic amplifier.

**O Saint Germain, what love you bring,
it truly makes all matter sing,
your violet flame does all restore,
with you we are becoming more.**

5. Saint Germain, send flood tides of Violet Flame to clear out the fear-based emotional vortexes that produce all kinds of envy, especially poverty.

O Saint Germain, I am now free,
your violet flame is therapy,
transform all hang-ups in my mind,
as inner peace I surely find.

**O Saint Germain, what love you bring,
it truly makes all matter sing,
your violet flame does all restore,
with you we are becoming more.**

6. Saint Germain, send flood tides of Violet Flame to clear out the fear-based emotional vortexes that produce illnesses, including a health-care industry driven by profit.

O Saint Germain, my body pure,
your violet flame for all is cure,
consume the cause of all disease,
and therefore I am all at ease.

**O Saint Germain, what love you bring,
it truly makes all matter sing,
your violet flame does all restore,
with you we are becoming more.**

7. Saint Germain, send flood tides of Violet Flame to clear out the fear-based emotional vortexes that produce political systems controlled by the special interest of various power elite groups.

O Saint Germain, I'm karma-free,
the past no longer burdens me,
a brand new opportunity,
I am in Christic unity.

**O Saint Germain, what love you bring,
it truly makes all matter sing,
your violet flame does all restore,
with you we are becoming more.**

8. Saint Germain, send flood tides of Violet Flame to clear out the fear-based emotional vortexes that produce religions that justify violence.

O Saint Germain, we are now one,
I am for you a violet sun,
as we transform this planet earth,
your Golden Age is given birth.

**O Saint Germain, what love you bring,
it truly makes all matter sing,
your violet flame does all restore,
with you we are becoming more.**

9. Saint Germain, send flood tides of Violet Flame to clear out the fear-based emotional vortexes that produce the subtle ignorance that dominates both mainstream religions, political systems and scientific materialism.

O Saint Germain, the earth is free,
from burden of duality,
in oneness we bring what is best,
your Golden Age is manifest.

**O Saint Germain, what love you bring,
it truly makes all matter sing,
your violet flame does all restore,
with you we are becoming more.**

Sealing

In the name of the I AM THAT I AM, the One Mind within me and within all life, I accept that Archangel Michael, Astrea and Shiva form an impenetrable shield around myself and all constructive people on earth, sealing us from all fear-based energies in all four octaves. I accept that the Light of God is consuming and transforming all fear-based energies on earth!

17 | INVOKING LIGHT INTO THE MENTAL OCTAVE

In the name of the I AM THAT I AM, the One Mind within me and within all life, I call upon Astrea to take command over the mental octave on earth and expose all false teachers. I call for Lord Maitreya to help all spiritual people awaken from the illusions that block our Divine plans. I call for Mother Mary to help us learn how to use the Ma-ter Light constructively. I call for Saint Germain to flood the mental octave with an irresistible surge of Violet Flame to transmute the energy veil that hides the false teachers. I especially call for Astrea, Maitreya, Mother Mary and Saint Germain to take command over …

[Make your own calls here.]

Part 1

1. Elohim Astrea, use your circle and sword to cut free myself and all constructive people from the false teachers in the mental octave.

> Astrea, loving Being white,
> your Presence is my pure delight,
> your sword and circle white and blue,
> the astral plane is cutting through.

> **Astrea, come accelerate,**
> **with purity I do vibrate,**
> **release the fire so blue and white,**
> **my aura filled with vibrant light.**

2. Elohim Astrea, use your circle and sword to cut free myself and all constructive people from the energy vortexes in the mental octave.

> Astrea, calm the raging storm,
> so purity will be the norm,
> my aura filled with blue and white,
> with shining armor, like a knight.

> **Astrea, come accelerate,**
> **with purity I do vibrate,**
> **release the fire so blue and white,**
> **my aura filled with vibrant light.**

17 | Invoking Light Into the Mental Octave

3. Elohim Astrea, use your circle and sword to cut free myself and all constructive people from the subtle illusions in the mental octave.

> Astrea, come and cut me free,
> from every binding entity,
> let astral forces all be bound,
> true freedom I have surely found.

> **Astrea, come accelerate,**
> **with purity I do vibrate,**
> **release the fire so blue and white,**
> **my aura filled with vibrant light.**

4. Elohim Astrea, use your circle and sword to clear the mental body of myself, all constructive people and the planet so the creative energies can flow through it freely.

> Astrea, I sincerely urge,
> from demons all, do me purge,
> consume them all and take me higher,
> I will endure your cleansing fire.

> **Astrea, come accelerate,**
> **with purity I do vibrate,**
> **release the fire so blue and white,**
> **my aura filled with vibrant light.**

5. Elohim Astrea, use your circle and sword to consume the energy vortexes used by the false teachers to justify war and violence against other people.

Astrea, do all spirits bind,
so that I am no longer blind,
I see the spirit and its twin,
the victory of Christ I win.

**Astrea, come accelerate,
with purity I do vibrate,
release the fire so blue and white,
my aura filled with vibrant light.**

6. Elohim Astrea, use your circle and sword to consume the energy vortexes used by the false teachers to justify war and violence against Mother Nature.

Astrea, clear my every cell,
from energies of death and hell,
my body is now free to grow,
each cell emits an inner glow.

**Astrea, come accelerate,
with purity I do vibrate,
release the fire so blue and white,
my aura filled with vibrant light.**

7. Elohim Astrea, use your circle and sword to consume the energy vortexes used by the false teachers to produce so many contradictory ideas that people do not know what to think.

Astrea, clear my feeling mind,
in purity my peace I find,
with higher feeling you release,
I co-create in perfect peace.

> Astrea, come accelerate,
> with purity I do vibrate,
> release the fire so blue and white,
> my aura filled with vibrant light.

8. Elohim Astrea, use your circle and sword to consume the energy vortexes used by the false teachers to make us follow them in their pursuit of some epic cause.

> Astrea, clear my mental realm,
> my Christ self always at the helm,
> I see now how to manifest,
> the matrix that for all is best.

> Astrea, come accelerate,
> with purity I do vibrate,
> release the fire so blue and white,
> my aura filled with vibrant light.

9. Elohim Astrea, use your circle and sword to consume the energy vortexes used by the false teachers to prevent us from tuning in to and accepting the guidance of the ascended masters.

> Astrea, with great clarity,
> I claim a new identity,
> etheric blueprint I now see,
> I co-create more consciously.

> Astrea, come accelerate,
> with purity I do vibrate,
> release the fire so blue and white,
> my aura filled with vibrant light.

Part 2

1. Lord Maitreya, awaken myself and all constructive people from the illusions used by the power elite to block the descent of a higher understanding of government.

> Maitreya, I am truly meek,
> your counsel wise I humbly seek,
> your vision I so want to see,
> with you in Eden I will be.
>
> **Maitreya, kindness is the cure,**
> **in fires of kindness I am pure.**
> **Maitreya, now release the fire,**
> **that raises me forever higher.**

2. Lord Maitreya, awaken myself and all constructive people from the illusions used by the power elite to block the descent of a higher understanding of education.

> Maitreya, help me to return,
> to learn from you, I truly yearn,
> as oneness is all I desire
> I feel initiation's fire.
>
> **Maitreya, kindness is the cure,**
> **in fires of kindness I am pure.**
> **Maitreya, now release the fire,**
> **that raises me forever higher.**

3. Lord Maitreya, awaken myself and all constructive people from the illusions used by the power elite to block the descent of a higher understanding of money systems and finance.

> Maitreya, I hereby decide,
> from you I will no longer hide,
> expose to me the very lie
> that caused edenic self to die.

> **Maitreya, kindness is the cure,**
> **in fires of kindness I am pure.**
> **Maitreya, now release the fire,**
> **that raises me forever higher.**

4. Lord Maitreya, awaken myself and all constructive people from the illusions used by the power elite to block the descent of a higher understanding of industry and business.

> Maitreya, blessed Guru mine,
> my heart of hearts forever thine,
> I vow that I will listen well,
> so we can break the serpent's spell.

> **Maitreya, kindness is the cure,**
> **in fires of kindness I am pure.**
> **Maitreya, now release the fire,**
> **that raises me forever higher.**

5. Lord Maitreya, awaken myself and all constructive people from the illusions used by the power elite to block the descent of a higher understanding of health and health care.

Maitreya, help me see the lie
whereby the serpent broke the tie,
the serpent now has naught in me,
in oneness I am truly free.

**Maitreya, kindness is the cure,
in fires of kindness I am pure.
Maitreya, now release the fire,
that raises me forever higher.**

6. Lord Maitreya, awaken myself and all constructive people from the illusions used by the power elite to block the descent of a higher understanding of religion and spirituality.

Maitreya, truth does set me free
from falsehoods of duality,
the fruit of knowledge I let go,
so your true spirit I do know.

**Maitreya, kindness is the cure,
in fires of kindness I am pure.
Maitreya, now release the fire,
that raises me forever higher.**

7. Lord Maitreya, awaken myself and all constructive people from the illusions used by the power elite to block the descent of a higher understanding of science and technology.

Maitreya, I submit to you,
intentions pure, my heart is true,
from ego I am truly free,
as I am now all one with thee.

17 | Invoking Light Into the Mental Octave

**Maitreya, kindness is the cure,
in fires of kindness I am pure.
Maitreya, now release the fire,
that raises me forever higher.**

8. Lord Maitreya, awaken myself and all constructive people from the illusions used by the power elite to block the descent of a higher understanding of new and unlimited sources of energy.

Maitreya, kindness is the key,
all shades of kindness teach to me,
for I am now the open door,
the Art of Kindness to restore.

**Maitreya, kindness is the cure,
in fires of kindness I am pure.
Maitreya, now release the fire,
that raises me forever higher.**

9. Lord Maitreya, awaken myself and all constructive people from the illusions used by the power elite to block the descent of a higher understanding of families and relationships.

Maitreya, oh sweet mystery,
immersed in your reality,
the myst'ry school will now return,
for this, my heart does truly burn.

**Maitreya, kindness is the cure,
in fires of kindness I am pure.
Maitreya, now release the fire,
that raises me forever higher.**

Part 3

1. Mother Mary, send the Mother Flame to consume the fear-based energies used by the power elite to block the descent of a higher understanding of our true roles a co-creators on earth.

> O blessed Mary, Mother mine,
> there is no greater love than thine,
> as we are one in heart and mind,
> my place in hierarchy I find.
>
> **O Mother Mary, generate,**
> **the song that does accelerate,**
> **the earth into a higher state,**
> **all matter does now scintillate.**

2. Mother Mary, send the Mother Flame to consume the fear-based energies used by the power elite to block the descent of a higher understanding of how to work with Mother Earth instead of seeking to fight her through force.

> I came to earth from heaven sent,
> as I am in embodiment,
> I use Divine authority,
> commanding you to set earth free.
>
> **O Mother Mary, generate,**
> **the song that does accelerate,**
> **the earth into a higher state,**
> **all matter does now scintillate.**

3. Mother Mary, send the Mother Flame to consume the fear-based energies used by the power elite to block the descent of a higher understanding of a non-violent way to interact with Mother Nature.

> I call now in God's sacred name,
> for you to use your Mother Flame,
> to burn all fear-based energy,
> restoring sacred harmony.

> **O Mother Mary, generate,**
> **the song that does accelerate,**
> **the earth into a higher state,**
> **all matter does now scintillate.**

4. Mother Mary, send the Mother Flame to consume the fear-based energies used by the power elite to block the descent of a higher understanding of how we can use our minds to get Mother Nature to manifest the abundant life for all people.

> Your sacred name I hereby praise,
> collective consciousness you raise,
> no more of fear and doubt and shame,
> consume it with your Mother Flame.

> **O Mother Mary, generate,**
> **the song that does accelerate,**
> **the earth into a higher state,**
> **all matter does now scintillate.**

5. Mother Mary, send the Mother Flame to consume the fear-based energies used by the power elite to block the descent of a higher understanding of new technologies that do not create pollution.

> All darkness from the earth you purge,
> your light moves as a mighty surge,
> no force of darkness can now stop,
> the spiral that goes only up.
>
> **O Mother Mary, generate,**
> **the song that does accelerate,**
> **the earth into a higher state,**
> **all matter does now scintillate.**

6. Mother Mary, send the Mother Flame to consume the fear-based energies used by the power elite to block the descent of a higher understanding of how to produce energy without using force.

> All elemental life you bless,
> removing from them man-made stress,
> the nature spirits are now free,
> outpicturing Divine decree.
>
> **O Mother Mary, generate,**
> **the song that does accelerate,**
> **the earth into a higher state,**
> **all matter does now scintillate.**

7. Mother Mary, send the Mother Flame to consume the fear-based energies used by the power elite to block the descent of a higher understanding of agriculture that will produce abundant food for all people.

> I raise my voice and take my stand,
> a stop to war I do command,
> no more shall warring scar the earth,
> a golden age is given birth.
>
> **O Mother Mary, generate,**
> **the song that does accelerate,**
> **the earth into a higher state,**
> **all matter does now scintillate.**

8. Mother Mary, send the Mother Flame to consume the fear-based energies used by the power elite to block the descent of a higher understanding of how to purify the earth from all man-made pollution, even emotional and mental pollution.

> As Mother Earth is free at last,
> disasters belong to the past,
> your Mother Light is so intense,
> that matter is now far less dense.
>
> **O Mother Mary, generate,**
> **the song that does accelerate,**
> **the earth into a higher state,**
> **all matter does now scintillate.**

9. Mother Mary, send the Mother Flame to consume the fear-based energies used by the power elite to block the descent of a higher understanding of how invoking spiritual light is the key to solving all problems.

> In Mother Light the earth is pure,
> the upward spiral will endure,
> prosperity is now the norm,
> God's vision manifest as form.
>
> **O Mother Mary, generate,**
> **the song that does accelerate,**
> **the earth into a higher state,**
> **all matter does now scintillate.**

Part 4

1. Saint Germain, send flood tides of Violet Flame to clear my own mental body and the mental bodies of all constructive people from all fear-based energy vortexes.

> O Saint Germain, you do inspire,
> my vision raised forever higher,
> with you I form a figure-eight,
> your Golden Age I co-create.
>
> **O Saint Germain, what love you bring,**
> **it truly makes all matter sing,**
> **your violet flame does all restore,**
> **with you we are becoming more.**

17 | Invoking Light Into the Mental Octave

2. Saint Germain, send flood tides of Violet Flame to clear the mental octave from the fear-based energy vortexes that impede the flow of creative energy.

> O Saint Germain, what Freedom Flame,
> released when we recite your name,
> acceleration is your gift,
> our planet it will surely lift.

> **O Saint Germain, what love you bring,**
> **it truly makes all matter sing,**
> **your violet flame does all restore,**
> **with you we are becoming more.**

3. Saint Germain, send flood tides of Violet Flame to consume the fear-based energy vortexes that hide the false teachers of the power elite and the forces behind them.

> O Saint Germain, in love we claim,
> our right to bring your violet flame,
> from you Above, to us below,
> it is an all-transforming flow.

> **O Saint Germain, what love you bring,**
> **it truly makes all matter sing,**
> **your violet flame does all restore,**
> **with you we are becoming more.**

4. Saint Germain, send flood tides of Violet Flame to consume the fear-based energy vortexes that prevent people from seeing through the illusions invented by the false teachers of the power elite.

O Saint Germain, I love you so,
my aura filled with violet glow,
my chakras filled with violet fire,
I am your cosmic amplifier.

**O Saint Germain, what love you bring,
it truly makes all matter sing,
your violet flame does all restore,
with you we are becoming more.**

5. Saint Germain, send flood tides of Violet Flame to consume the fear-based energy vortexes that block the vision of your golden age.

O Saint Germain, I am now free,
your violet flame is therapy,
transform all hang-ups in my mind,
as inner peace I surely find.

**O Saint Germain, what love you bring,
it truly makes all matter sing,
your violet flame does all restore,
with you we are becoming more.**

6. Saint Germain, send flood tides of Violet Flame to consume the fear-based energy vortexes that block the vision of how constructive people can help manifest your golden age.

O Saint Germain, my body pure,
your violet flame for all is cure,
consume the cause of all disease,
and therefore I am all at ease.

**O Saint Germain, what love you bring,
it truly makes all matter sing,
your violet flame does all restore,
with you we are becoming more.**

7. Saint Germain, send flood tides of Violet Flame to consume the fear-based energy vortexes that block the vision of why we volunteered to embody at this time in order to help manifest your golden age.

O Saint Germain, I'm karma-free,
the past no longer burdens me,
a brand new opportunity,
I am in Christic unity.

**O Saint Germain, what love you bring,
it truly makes all matter sing,
your violet flame does all restore,
with you we are becoming more.**

8. Saint Germain, send flood tides of Violet Flame to consume the fear-based energy vortexes that block the vision of how a new approach to religion can help manifest your golden age.

O Saint Germain, we are now one,
I am for you a violet sun,
as we transform this planet earth,
your Golden Age is given birth.

**O Saint Germain, what love you bring,
it truly makes all matter sing,
your violet flame does all restore,
with you we are becoming more.**

9. Saint Germain, send flood tides of Violet Flame to consume the fear-based energy vortexes that block the vision of how a new approach to science can help manifest your golden age.

> O Saint Germain, the earth is free,
> from burden of duality,
> in oneness we bring what is best,
> your Golden Age is manifest.
>
> **O Saint Germain, what love you bring,**
> **it truly makes all matter sing,**
> **your violet flame does all restore,**
> **with you we are becoming more.**

Sealing

In the name of the I AM THAT I AM, the One Mind within me and within all life, I accept that Archangel Michael, Astrea and Shiva form an impenetrable shield around myself and all constructive people on earth, sealing us from all fear-based energies in all four octaves. I accept that the Light of God is consuming and transforming all fear-based energies on earth!

18 | INVOKING LIGHT INTO THE IDENTITY OCTAVE

In the name of the I AM THAT I AM, the One Mind within me and within all life, I call upon Jesus, Lord Maitreya, Gautama Buddha and Sanat Kumara to consume all fear-based energy vortexes in the identity octave on earth. Use your ruby ray fire to consume the energy veil that keeps people trapped in a false sense of identity. I especially call for you to take command over …

[Make your own calls here.]

Part 1

1. Beloved Jesus, send the Christ light into the identity octave and awaken myself and all constructive people so we can accept you as an example and accept our right and potential to follow your example.

O Jesus, blessed brother mine,
I walk the path that you outline,
a great example to us all,
I follow now your inner call.

**O Jesus, let the Fire of Joy,
consume the devil's subtle ploy,
transfigured is our planet earth,
the golden age is given birth.**

2. Beloved Jesus, send the Christ light into the identity octave and awaken myself and all constructive people so we can accept that we are all sons and daughters of God.

O Jesus, open inner sight,
the ego wants to prove it's right,
but this I will no longer do,
I want to be all one with you.

**O Jesus, let the Fire of Joy,
consume the devil's subtle ploy,
transfigured is our planet earth,
the golden age is given birth.**

3. Beloved Jesus, send the Christ light into the identity octave and awaken myself and all constructive people so we can accept that we all have the potential to manifest Christhood and thereby challenge the power elite as you did.

O Jesus, I now clearly see,
the Key of Knowledge given me,
my Christ self I hereby embrace,
as you fill up my inner space.

18 | Invoking Light Into the Identity Octave

**O Jesus, let the Fire of Joy,
consume the devil's subtle ploy,
transfigured is our planet earth,
the golden age is given birth.**

4. Beloved Jesus, send the Christ light into the identity octave and awaken myself and all constructive people so we can accept our right and our potential to challenge the power elite in the area of religion.

O Jesus, show me serpent's lie,
expose the beam in my own eye,
as Christ discernment you me give,
in oneness I forever live.

**O Jesus, let the Fire of Joy,
consume the devil's subtle ploy,
transfigured is our planet earth,
the golden age is given birth.**

5. Beloved Jesus, send the Christ light into the identity octave and awaken myself and all constructive people so we can accept our right and our potential to challenge the power elite in the area of government.

O Jesus, I am truly meek,
and thus I turn the other cheek,
when the accuser attacks me,
I go within and merge with thee.

> **O Jesus, let the Fire of Joy,**
> **consume the devil's subtle ploy,**
> **transfigured is our planet earth,**
> **the golden age is given birth.**

6. Beloved Jesus, send the Christ light into the identity octave and awaken myself and all constructive people so we can accept our right and our potential to challenge the power elite in the area of science.

> O Jesus, ego I let die,
> surrender ev'ry earthly tie,
> the dead can bury what is dead,
> I choose to walk with you instead.

> **O Jesus, let the Fire of Joy,**
> **consume the devil's subtle ploy,**
> **transfigured is our planet earth,**
> **the golden age is given birth.**

7. Beloved Jesus, send the Christ light into the identity octave and awaken myself and all constructive people so we can accept our right and our potential to challenge the power elite in the area of education.

> O Jesus, help me rise above,
> the devil's test through higher love,
> show me separate self unreal,
> my formless self you do reveal.

**O Jesus, let the Fire of Joy,
consume the devil's subtle ploy,
transfigured is our planet earth,
the golden age is given birth.**

8. Beloved Jesus, send the Christ light into the identity octave and awaken myself and all constructive people so we can accept our right and our potential to challenge the power elite in the area of business and finance.

O Jesus, what is that to me,
I just let go and follow thee,
with this I do pass ev'ry test,
to find with you eternal rest.

**O Jesus, let the Fire of Joy,
consume the devil's subtle ploy,
transfigured is our planet earth,
the golden age is given birth.**

9. Beloved Jesus, send the Christ light into the identity octave and awaken myself and all constructive people so we can accept our right and our potential to challenge the power elite in the area of justice and the courts.

O Jesus, fiery master mine,
my heart now melting into thine,
I love with heart and mind and soul,
the God who is my highest goal.

> O Jesus, let the Fire of Joy,
> consume the devil's subtle ploy,
> transfigured is our planet earth,
> the golden age is given birth.

Part 2

1. Lord Maitreya, I call forth the awakening of all constructive people who have the potential to bring forth new ideas in the areas of religion and spirituality.

> Maitreya, I am truly meek,
> your counsel wise I humbly seek,
> your vision I so want to see,
> with you in Eden I will be.

> **Maitreya, kindness is the cure,**
> **in fires of kindness I am pure.**
> **Maitreya, now release the fire,**
> **that raises me forever higher.**

2. Lord Maitreya, I call forth the awakening of all constructive people who have the potential to bring forth new ideas in the areas of government and justice.

> Maitreya, help me to return,
> to learn from you, I truly yearn,
> as oneness is all I desire
> I feel initiation's fire.

**Maitreya, kindness is the cure,
in fires of kindness I am pure.
Maitreya, now release the fire,
that raises me forever higher.**

3. Lord Maitreya, I call forth the awakening of all constructive people who have the potential to bring forth new ideas in the areas of money and finance.

Maitreya, I hereby decide,
from you I will no longer hide,
expose to me the very lie
that caused edenic self to die.

**Maitreya, kindness is the cure,
in fires of kindness I am pure.
Maitreya, now release the fire,
that raises me forever higher.**

4. Lord Maitreya, I call forth the awakening of all constructive people who have the potential to bring forth new ideas in the areas of business and agriculture

Maitreya, blessed Guru mine,
my heart of hearts forever thine,
I vow that I will listen well,
so we can break the serpent's spell.

**Maitreya, kindness is the cure,
in fires of kindness I am pure.
Maitreya, now release the fire,
that raises me forever higher.**

5. Lord Maitreya, I call forth the awakening of all constructive people who have the potential to bring forth new ideas in the areas of education and the media.

> Maitreya, help me see the lie
> whereby the serpent broke the tie,
> the serpent now has naught in me,
> in oneness I am truly free.
>
> **Maitreya, kindness is the cure,**
> **in fires of kindness I am pure.**
> **Maitreya, now release the fire,**
> **that raises me forever higher.**

6. Lord Maitreya, I call forth the awakening of all constructive people who have the potential to bring forth new ideas in the areas of science and technology.

> Maitreya, truth does set me free
> from falsehoods of duality,
> the fruit of knowledge I let go,
> so your true spirit I do know.
>
> **Maitreya, kindness is the cure,**
> **in fires of kindness I am pure.**
> **Maitreya, now release the fire,**
> **that raises me forever higher.**

7. Lord Maitreya, I call forth the awakening of all constructive people who have the potential to bring forth new ideas in the areas of health care and families.

Maitreya, I submit to you,
intentions pure, my heart is true,
from ego I am truly free,
as I am now all one with thee.

Maitreya, kindness is the cure,
in fires of kindness I am pure.
Maitreya, now release the fire,
that raises me forever higher.

8. Lord Maitreya, I call forth the awakening of all constructive people who have the potential to bring forth new ideas in the areas of our relationship with Mother Earth.

Maitreya, kindness is the key,
all shades of kindness teach to me,
for I am now the open door,
the Art of Kindness to restore.

Maitreya, kindness is the cure,
in fires of kindness I am pure.
Maitreya, now release the fire,
that raises me forever higher.

9. Lord Maitreya, I call forth the awakening of all constructive people who have the potential to bring forth new ideas in the areas of energy technology, both production and distribution.

Maitreya, oh sweet mystery,
immersed in your reality,
the myst'ry school will now return,
for this, my heart does truly burn.

> **Maitreya, kindness is the cure,**
> **in fires of kindness I am pure.**
> **Maitreya, now release the fire,**
> **that raises me forever higher.**

Part 3

1. Gautama Buddha, I call forth the awakening of all constructive people who have the potential to bring forth an awareness of how to transcend conflict and bring true peace.

> Gautama, show my mental state
> that does give rise to love and hate,
> your exposé I do endure,
> so my perception will be pure.
>
> **Gautama, Flame of Cosmic Peace,**
> **unruly thoughts do hereby cease,**
> **we radiate from you and me**
> **the peace to still Samsara's Sea.**

2. Gautama Buddha, I call forth the awakening of all constructive people who have the potential to bring forth an awareness of how we have become trapped in a dualistic state of consciousness that is the cause of all conflict.

> Gautama, in your Flame of Peace,
> the struggling self I now release,
> the Buddha Nature I now see,
> it is the core of you and me.

> **Gautama, Flame of Cosmic Peace,
> unruly thoughts do hereby cease,
> we radiate from you and me
> the peace to still Samsara's Sea.**

3. Gautama Buddha, I call forth the awakening of all constructive people who have the potential to bring forth an awareness of how the members of the power elite are using the duality consciousness to control the population.

> Gautama, I am one with thee,
> Mara's demons do now flee,
> your Presence like a soothing balm,
> my mind and senses ever calm.

> **Gautama, Flame of Cosmic Peace,
> unruly thoughts do hereby cease,
> we radiate from you and me
> the peace to still Samsara's Sea.**

4. Gautama Buddha, I call forth the awakening of all constructive people who have the potential to bring forth an awareness of how the duality consciousness causes us to generate conflicts and wars that we cannot see how to stop.

> Gautama, I now take the vow,
> to live in the eternal now,
> with you I do transcend all time,
> to live in present so sublime.

**Gautama, Flame of Cosmic Peace,
unruly thoughts do hereby cease,
we radiate from you and me
the peace to still Samsara's Sea.**

5. Gautama Buddha, I call forth the awakening of all constructive people who have the potential to bring forth an awareness of how the duality consciousness causes us to be unable to see each other as spiritual beings coming from the same source.

> Gautama, I have no desire,
> to nothing earthly I aspire,
> in non-attachment I now rest,
> passing Mara's subtle test.

**Gautama, Flame of Cosmic Peace,
unruly thoughts do hereby cease,
we radiate from you and me
the peace to still Samsara's Sea.**

6. Gautama Buddha, I call forth the awakening of all constructive people who have the potential to bring forth an awareness of how the duality consciousness enables us to camouflage self-interest as serving a cause of epic importance.

> Gautama, I melt into you,
> my mind is one, no longer two,
> immersed in your resplendent glow,
> Nirvana is all that I know.

**Gautama, Flame of Cosmic Peace,
unruly thoughts do hereby cease,
we radiate from you and me
the peace to still Samsara's Sea.**

7. Gautama Buddha, I call forth the awakening of all constructive people who have the potential to bring forth an awareness of how the duality consciousness becomes a closed system by enabling us to justify anything we want.

Gautama, in your timeless space,
I am immersed in Cosmic Grace,
I know the God beyond all form,
to world I will no more conform.

**Gautama, Flame of Cosmic Peace,
unruly thoughts do hereby cease,
we radiate from you and me
the peace to still Samsara's Sea.**

8. Gautama Buddha, I call forth the awakening of all constructive people who have the potential to bring forth an awareness of how the duality consciousness keeps us separated from each other, Mother Nature, the ascended masters and God.

Gautama, I am now awake,
I clearly see what is at stake,
and thus I claim my sacred right
to be on earth the Buddhic Light.

**Gautama, Flame of Cosmic Peace,
unruly thoughts do hereby cease,
we radiate from you and me
the peace to still Samsara's Sea.**

9. Gautama Buddha, I call forth the awakening of all constructive people who have the potential to bring forth an awareness of how the duality consciousness prevents us from accepting who we are and why we are in embodiment on earth at this particular time.

> Gautama, with your thunderbolt,
> we give the earth a mighty jolt,
> I know that some will understand,
> and join the Buddha's timeless band.

**Gautama, Flame of Cosmic Peace,
unruly thoughts do hereby cease,
we radiate from you and me
the peace to still Samsara's Sea.**

Part 4

1. Sanat Kumara, I call forth the awakening of all constructive people who have the potential to expose power elite groups and how they have used religion to gain power over the people.

> Sanat Kumara, Ruby Fire,
> I seek my place in love's own choir,
> with open hearts we sing your praise,
> together we the earth do raise.

18 | Invoking Light Into the Identity Octave

> **Sanat Kumara, Ruby Ray,**
> **bring to earth a higher way,**
> **light this planet with your fire,**
> **clothe her in a new attire.**

2. Sanat Kumara, I call forth the awakening of all constructive people who have the potential to expose power elite groups and how they have used science to gain power over the people.

> Sanat Kumara, Ruby Fire,
> initiations I desire,
> I am for you an electrode,
> Shamballa is my true abode.

> **Sanat Kumara, Ruby Ray,**
> **bring to earth a higher way,**
> **light this planet with your fire,**
> **clothe her in a new attire.**

3. Sanat Kumara, I call forth the awakening of all constructive people who have the potential to expose power elite groups and how they have used government to gain power over the people.

> Sanat Kumara, Ruby Fire,
> I follow path that you require,
> initiate me with your love,
> the open door for Holy Dove.

> **Sanat Kumara, Ruby Ray,**
> **bring to earth a higher way,**
> **light this planet with your fire,**
> **clothe her in a new attire.**

4. Sanat Kumara, I call forth the awakening of all constructive people who have the potential to expose power elite groups and how they have used the military to gain power over the people.

> Sanat Kumara, Ruby Fire,
> your great example all inspire,
> with non-attachment and great mirth,
> we give the earth a true rebirth.
>
> **Sanat Kumara, Ruby Ray,**
> **bring to earth a higher way,**
> **light this planet with your fire,**
> **clothe her in a new attire.**

5. Sanat Kumara, I call forth the awakening of all constructive people who have the potential to expose power elite groups and how they have used education to gain power over the people.

> Sanat Kumara, Ruby Fire,
> you are this planet's purifier,
> consume on earth all spirits dark,
> reveal the inner Spirit Spark.
>
> **Sanat Kumara, Ruby Ray,**
> **bring to earth a higher way,**
> **light this planet with your fire,**
> **clothe her in a new attire.**

6. Sanat Kumara, I call forth the awakening of all constructive people who have the potential to expose power elite groups and how they have used the media to gain power over the people.

> Sanat Kumara, Ruby Fire,
> you are a cosmic amplifier,
> the lower forces can't withstand,
> vibrations from Venusian band.

> **Sanat Kumara, Ruby Ray,**
> **bring to earth a higher way,**
> **light this planet with your fire,**
> **clothe her in a new attire.**

7. Sanat Kumara, I call forth the awakening of all constructive people who have the potential to expose power elite groups and how they have used money to gain power over the people.

> Sanat Kumara, Ruby Fire,
> I am on earth your magnifier,
> the flow of love I do restore,
> my chakras are your open door.

> **Sanat Kumara, Ruby Ray,**
> **bring to earth a higher way,**
> **light this planet with your fire,**
> **clothe her in a new attire.**

8. Sanat Kumara, I call forth the awakening of all constructive people who have the potential to expose power elite groups and how they have used business to gain power over the people.

Sanat Kumara, Ruby Fire,
Venusian song the multiplier,
as we your love reverberate,
the densest minds we penetrate.

**Sanat Kumara, Ruby Ray,
bring to earth a higher way,
light this planet with your fire,
clothe her in a new attire.**

9. Sanat Kumara, I call forth the awakening of all constructive people who have the potential to expose power elite groups and how they have used health care to gain power over the people.

Sanat Kumara, Ruby Fire,
you are for all the sanctifier
the earth is now a holy place,
purified by cosmic grace.

**Sanat Kumara, Ruby Ray,
bring to earth a higher way,
light this planet with your fire,
clothe her in a new attire.**

Sealing

In the name of the I AM THAT I AM, the One Mind within me and within all life, I accept that Archangel Michael, Astrea and Shiva form an impenetrable shield around myself and all constructive people on earth, sealing us from all fear-based energies in all four octaves. I accept that the Light of God is consuming and transforming all fear-based energies on earth!

www.ingramcontent.com/pod-product-compliance
Lightning Source LLC
Chambersburg PA
CBHW030105170426
43198CB00009B/503